Belt and Road vs. China and the World:

Perspectives of the Chinese

Modern China Series

Belt and Road vs. China and the World:

Perspectives of the Chinese

Tian Guang
Chen Gang

North American Business Press

Belt and Road vs. China and the World: Perspectives of the Chinese

ISBN: 978-1-948915-16-8

NORTH AMERICAN BUSINESS PRESS

North American Business Press
Atlanta, Georgia
Miami, Florida
New York, New York,
Toronto, Canada

FIRST PRINTING, 2020

About Modern China Series

China, as one of the oldest civilized regions in the world, has emerged as something of a "new world" because it is working to embrace its essence and heritage and link them to viable economic strategies. In the last 25 years, China has made tremendous strides by doing so. The country and her people have every right to take pride in these accomplishments. With these successes under their belt, many Chinese leaders and intellectuals anticipate continuing growth. China's plans and strategies, furthermore, are often based upon this premise.

There is tremendous interest in the US on the Chinese economy and business environment. China has emerged as a global superpower, and scholars and business people in the US are keenly interested in learning how this is going to continue to affect them and how they can do business with China. In response to growing interest from international and Asian scholars, North American Business Press is pleased to announce our Modern China Series (MCS) books. It is the first book series about modern China in the US, which has garnered tremendous interest both in the US and around the world. With our first book reaching stores in September 2011, this initiative is aimed at developing relationships between NABP and Chinese scholars. They desire to promote their academic and applied business writings to the rest of the world.

We have had an overwhelming demand for the Modern China Series from both authors who would like to publish in the series and people who would like to read the books. Currently, there are ten books published in the series, and, additionally, we have a couple of dozen books that we are considering for the series. The books have been viewed by tens of thousands of people from the U.S. and the rest of the world.

We have published books relating to several areas revolving around the Chinese business environment. We have a few that focus on the best practices in marketing in China; some are comparing to "best practices" in doing business in China, and a few on the outlook of the Chinese economy. The market for the Modern China Series is enormous. There are tens of thousands of scholars that are keenly interested in the continued growth of the Chinese economy and the implications that will have on the business world. Even more significant are the millions of business people that are interested in the impact that China will continue to have on the global economy. It is difficult to pin down the exact demand for the series, but it Is enormous.

We have big plans for growing the Modern China Series. It has the potential to be one of the most significant economic/business series ever produced. We are very selective with the books that we will add to the collection, but we encourage any scholars who think they have unique and exciting perspectives on China to submit their book manuscripts to us. From the readers' perspective, we are committed to producing high-quality books regularly so that readers should expect a steady stream of insightful books to be coming out for many years to come.

This initiative is headed by Dr. Robert Tian, a renowned researcher and academic, who spearheads our efforts in partnering with foreign authors and administering day-to-day operations of this series. Dr. Tian, a Vice-President with North American Business Press and Editor of this series, spends much of his time in Beijing, Shanghai, and other Chinese cities, focusing on developing and managing our interests with authors and universities. Below is the list for the books we have published:

Enterprise Strategy: New Horizon authored by Zhang Xiuyu
Governance of Private Enterprises in Modern China authored by Zhong Qin
The Art of War and Enterprise Strategy Management authored by Fu Shouzhi
Marketing Issues in Modern China edited by Robert Guang Tian et al.
The Footprints of the Academician authored by Fu Zhouzhi

Marketing and Economics in Modern China (I) edited by Xiaoguang Qi et al.
Marketing and Economics in Modern China (II) edited by Wang Tianjin et al.
An Islamic Heritage in China authored by Ma Zhanming
China Environmental Anthropology authored by Wang Tianjin, Tian Guang, and Ma Jianfu
Can China Rule the New World? Authored by Tian Guang and Chen Gang
Critiques on Pan-marketization authored by Li Cunlin, Liu Hongfei, and Tian Guang
Economic and Business Anthropology in China edited by Xiaoguang Qi and Tian Guang
China-Mongolia Economic Corridor authored by Eerdun Taoketao, Zhang Zhe, Wang Gang, and Wei Lisi
Anthropology of Chinese Foodways authored by Tian Guang and Chen Gang
Urbanization of Rural China authored by Li Taohong
Child Rearing in Rural China by Jiang Youchun and Yang Yunyi
Belt and Road vs. China and World by Tian Guang and Chen Gang

Table of Contents

Preface

The One' Belt One Road initiative is a historical initiative that connects the people over the world and facilitates various opportunities for global peace. Our primary purpose in editing this book is to explore the implication of One Belt One Road initiative for global future development. We aimed at analyzing the reasons of origin, strategy, opportunities and challenges of One Belt One Road initiatives based on business, economic, political, social and environmental aspects by inventorying the literature that focused on the current progress of One Belt One Road. Some scholars argue that partner countries and agencies of One Belt One Road will get economic and political benefits from these initiatives. It facilitates connecting people through roadways, airways and waterways, coordinating policies of various governments, financial integration through cross border business, productivity and regional energy security. Based on our inventory of the literature, we also outlined the risks and challenges associated with One Belt One Road initiative implementation. It suggests that strong coordination among partners of One Belt One Road is necessary to get full fruits of One Belt One Road through supportive law, policy, rules and regulations, proper strategy implementation, transparent procurement the system, sincere consideration on political, financial, environmental and social factors.

Chinese President Xi Jinping proposed the One Belt One Road initiative in 2013. It is a historical initiative of China to connect people all over the world. Recently it is known as Belt and Road Initiative. It comprises two significant programs entitled to Silk Road Economic Belt and 21st Century Maritime Silk Road. The Silk Road Economic Belt connects three major routes like China to Europe, the Persian Gulf, the Mediterranean and the Indian Ocean. At the same time, the 21st Century Maritime Silk Road is based on waterways among member countries of the One Belt One Road initiative. It comprises about 65 countries and 900 projects with an investment volume of 850 billion dollars. The Asian Infrastructure Investment Bank (AIIB) was launched with its startup capital of 100 billion dollars in the context of One Belt One Road.

The One Belt denotes the "Silk Road Economic Belt," a revival of the old land-based Silk Road, which connected China to Central Asia, The Middle East and Europe. So, it is also known as Modern Silk Road. It also denotes the "21st Century Maritime Silk Road," which planned to connect Asia, Africa, the Middle East and Europe. It is also known as Maritime Silk Road. The One Belt One Road aims to connect Asia, Europe and Africa through strengthening partnerships among the countries.

China's imperial envoy Zhang Qian initiated the old Silk Road 2000 years ago, which has been facilitated as a trade route to Arab and central Asia. Since silk was one of the first export items of china at that time so this route is known as Silk Road. In 2013, President Xi Jinping declared to establish and revitalize the old Silk Road by creating a connection among China, all parts of Asia, Europe and Africa through infrastructure development like railways and roads. It is the most significant economic platform in the world, which will promote global economic growth through strengthening economic cooperation. One Belt One Road is working in two ways viz. Silk Road Economic Belt and 21st Century Maritime Silk Road. The Silk Road Economic Belt consists of three routes connecting China to Europe, the Persian Gulf, the Mediterranean and the Indian Ocean.

On the other hand, the 21st Century Maritime Silk The road is based on waterways among One Belt One Road member countries. One Belt One Road is a mega project which covers two-thirds of the global population and three-fourth of the energy resources. Though some researchers thought that One Belt One Road is an initiative to promote their meltdown economy by creating smooth global markets, it is portrayed to reshape the political and economic order of Asia by developing a network of cultural, political and trading corporations. The

One Belt One Road already got Sixty-five countries as members under its initiative.

The importance of the One Belt One Road initiative cannot be ignored due to its active role in mutual peace and economic development. It connects Asian countries like Bangladesh, Brunei, Singapore, Sri Lanka, Cambodia, Myanmar, Maldives, Nepal, India, Sudan and Pakistan through seaports, oil and gas pipelines and economic corridors. It also finances for free trade economic zones and energy development projects in its member countries. The policymakers and scholars of the US, Japan and India, expressed their security threats in the One Belt One Road regions due to the growing influence of the One Belt One Road initiative of China.

Though China considered it as propaganda against One Belt One Road's peaceful journey, the benefit of the One Belt One Road will be available for all the people of the world due to its friendly natures like cooperation, integration and interdependence. A multi-polar world will be established by the proper implementation of One Belt One Road through trends of harmony and peace. Many studies analyzed the suitability of One Belt One Road for the future of global development in terms of economic sustainability, political stability and cultural exchange. Some scholars argue that the One Belt One Road initiative has great potential for the future of global growth. It also analyzes the context of origin, vision, strategy, challenges and opportunities of the One Belt One Road initiative considering its applicability for global development.

Some scholars argue that China has a significant influence on the One Belt One Road initiative as an initiator and encouraging China's Go-West policy at all. Still, it has a good impact on the economy of its partner as a whole. The shreds of evidence indicate some significant challenges of One Belt One Road like sheer size and scale, massive infrastructure development, various geography and topography, geographical problems and security challenges within the region. We suggest that strong coordination among partners of One Belt One Road is necessary to get full fruits of One Belt One Road through supportive law, policy, rules and regulations, proper strategy implementation, transparent procurement system, sincere consideration on political, financial, environmental and social factors.

The One Belt One Road initiative not only enhanced the fast development of China but also generated an impact on the world's political and economic patterns. Some American political leaders believe that China's aggressive and robust rise is to replace the United States' leading position in the world. However, Chinese scholars believe that in China, there may be a very few, but absolutely not dominant, among the top leaders think so, and this idea does not have any realistic possibility. The reasons are as follows: first, Chinese is not the international language; second, RMB is not an international currency; third, China cannot deliver military power to the world; fourth, China cannot provide a series of public goods to the world; fifth, most countries in the world do not recognize China's current system and values, as such there is no real ally for China; sixth, China's economy ranks second in the world in terms of appearance and essence, the dazzling total amount divided by 1.4 billion denominators will rank behind in the world; seventh, the contradictions accumulated in China's rapid growth in recent decades are mostly suppressed by "maintaining stability" and have not yet been resolved. Finally, education in China is rigid and ideological suffocation leads to science and technology learning without thickness, good at imitating the first-class but poor in innovation, lack of long-distance running endurance. Therefore, China cannot be the leader of the global village (Weng, 2018).

As to the United States, Chinese scholars believe that the United States is at the peak of its development, and it usually goes downhill when it reaches its peak. However, the peak of the United States is not mounting Everest, but it is in a flat top of the mountain. It may take a long time for the United States to go through this flat top of the mountain. Therefore, the United States can continue to be the leader of the world. However, the United States also has two key issues to pay attention to: first, the United States may not replace international law with its domestic law; second, the United States should consult with others when there are somethings must be done, and it is better not to act arbitrarily (Weng, 2018).

Our book contributes to the ongoing debate on the positive and negative effect of the One Belt One Road initiative by exploring the context of origin, strategy, challenges, opportunities and implications for global future development. We have adopted a qualitative approach to preparing the manuscript by collecting and presenting secondary data, mainly journal articles, conference proceedings, various documents of government, books, newspaper articles, magazine articles, and multiple websites of the internet. Although we need to take responsibility for the contents contained in this book, we must declare that all the arguments and statements we presented in the book are totally and absolutely from the Chinese scholars and leaderships. As such, it is necessary to indicate that our contributions are mainly limited to comb and present these arguments and statements in a way that the western people can read and understand them in English.

Foreword 1

Russell Belk

The Belt and Road Initiative is a project of such historical, cultural, geographic, economic, and strategic significance that it is impossible to describe and analyze in a single volume thoroughly. This book makes no pretense of doing that. As the subtitle suggests, it presents a Chinese perspective by a scholar whose life has been spent between China, the United States, and Canada. Together with his anthropological credentials, this places Robert Tian in a unique position to clarify the Chinese government's and Chinese people's perspectives on this grand project. His collaboration with Chen Gang deepens and magnifies the Chinese perspective.

The oft-made comparison to the Marshall Plan implemented by the U.S. after World War II is useful, despite the many differences between the two initiatives as outlined by Tian and Chen and as discussed by Alf Walle in his Forward. Both were or are planned by rising world powers to solidify allegiances with nation-states that could assure their ultimate power and security. But whereas the U.S. was seeking to reanimate the well-developed if war-ravished states of Western Europe, the Chinese are seeking to animate the less-developed if war-torn states of Africa, the Middle East, parts of Europe, and parts of Asia. Moreover, the cultures of the countries touched by the Belt and Road are vastly different not only from China but also from each other. However, the realignment of regional loyalties due to financial and political entanglements is similar to the obligations the U.S. sought to build with Western Europe in its Cold War with the Soviet Union and its satellite states in Eastern Europe, Asia, and Cuba.

Perhaps a more apt analogy than the Marshall Plan might be the spread of European colonialism in the nineteenth and early twentieth centuries. In these more aggressive forays, European states launched initiatives into Africa, the Caribbean, and Asia in an effort that was, in some cases, nearly as exploitative as slavery – an institution with which it overlapped. The Chinese B&R initiative is not aggressive or religious as were most European colonialist exploits, and it does not attempt to take control of any of the nations involved. As Tian and Chen rightly emphasize, it uses soft power and digital, monetary, and commercial means to extend its influence. But make no mistake, the B&R is not motivated by pure altruism. This great initiative is shaping the future world order at a time when it appears that the U.S. and China are on the brink of entering a Cold War.

Interesting comparisons might be made between the B&R initiative and the way China is dealing with cultural and political conflicts within Asia. This includes its dealings with Hong Kong, Tibet, Xinjiang, the South China Seas, Taiwan, and India. Soft power only goes so far. Military, police, internment/re-education, investment, Han settlers, diplomacy, propaganda, surveillance, and industrial development are all among the techniques used in these cases. There is some overlap with the techniques used in the B&R, especially investment, diplomacy, industrial development, and propaganda. But it is not far-fetched to wonder whether others of these techniques may be employed in the future.

This may sound like a more Western perspective than the Chinese Perspective delivered so well here. It is also speculative about how the battle for global dominance may play out with an ascendant China and a declining America. Still, I think it appropriately raises a more aggressive possible future scenario than seen in some parts of the book. For instance, the book states that:

> *The goal of the socialist market economy is to ensure that the country is prosperous, and the people are well-off and healthy with better rights and interests, and that all Chinese people live in a safe and beautiful countryside.*

Except for better rights and interests, I do not doubt that this is true, if for no other reason than that these conditions are necessary for political stability within China. But what I am trying to suggest is that in order to achieve these goals for China and Chinese people, it may be necessary to compromise on achieving some of these goals for those in countries through which the Belt and Road and Maritime Silk Road initiatives pass.

Much is at stake here. These initiatives involve more than 60 countries and two-thirds of the world's population. They also affect the health of the Chinese economy. And the Belt and Road and Maritime Silk Road initiatives can potentially create an economic boom in all parts of the world. The global financial crisis of 2008 and the COVID-19 pandemic of 2020 have been barriers to their progress, but not insurmountable roadblocks. Indebted both economically and morally, the nations directly affected will tell the tale. Can the B&R tide lift all ships? Could it sink some ships? We shall see. The ideas discussed here offer some insights.

Foreword 2

Alf Walle

China's Belt and Road Initiative is the attempt by China to construct an infrastructure and transportation network stretching from Asia to the Middle East, to Africa and ultimately to Europe. Currently, it is employing Chinese construction workers and contracts to Chinese companies. In the process, participating countries and regions are becoming indebted to China as infrastructures are built that are designed to provide economic advantages and benefits to China. If successful, the Belt and Road initiative will be a catalyst for China's economic and cultural hegemony in ways that potentially preempt the West and the United States from having full access to these regions and their markets. Because the peoples and neighborhoods being served are destined to rise in importance during the 21st century, the Belt and Road have long term implications that scholars, practitioners, and strategists need to consider and address.

As a result, Western researchers, practitioners, and strategists need to be aware of the Belt and Road and its potentials in order to understand better how China is orchestrating strategies that possess long term implications. This volume provides insights in this regard. It is written by Dr. Guang Tian (a longtime colleague and sometimes collaborator who I have known for over 20 years) and Dr. Gang Chen. Dr. Tian is an American who was born and raised in China and taught business in the USA and China for many years; Tian is recognized as a major business anthropologist. As a result, he is uniquely qualified to head this project.

Although Tian possesses a unique understanding of the Belt and Road, unavoidable circumstances have prevented his analysis from being fully edited in a genuinely academic fashion. This is because Tian is currently suffering from significant eyesight difficulties. As a result, the reader might notice problems in the presentation that sometimes make it difficult to perceive if Tian is stating his opinion, as a scholar, or if he is seeking to portray the thinking of Chinese strategists who are apologists for the Belt and Road Initiative. But, as the old saying goes, "being forewarned is forearmed." If readers are aware of these issues of communication and interpret the text accordingly, much can be gained from this book.

Faced with a publication decision, the authors had two possibilities. The first would have been to delay publication indefinitely until Tian's eyesight improves, and his ability to edit returns fully. Doing so would have resulted in a "better" product but would have kept their message from the reader for an extended period. The alternative is to publish in a timely manner in order to make their observations available when needed, even if certain limitations exist in the presentation. The authors had chosen the latter strategy. I understand their thinking, and I hope the reader does too. Read from this perspective, the reader can profit from the book.

Much of the first chapter can be read as the Chinese leadership justifying its actions as altruistic. Thus, we are told that "Construction of the Belt and Road Initiative is a demonstration of Chinese cultural value featured by openness, inclusiveness, peace and amicability." Although this might be true to a degree, the Chinese also appear to be seeking to expand its sphere of influence, develop a higher degree of cultural and economic hegemony, and deter future Western attempts to do business over a significant part of the world. Nevertheless, such discussions are useful because they provide an understanding of how the Chinese leadership thinks (or at least how it seeks to portray and justify the Belt and Road).

Chapter 1 also provides an analysis of the post-World War 2 Marshal Plan that helped rebuild wore torn Europe. Consider the following quotation:

> *The domestic media is more likely to believe that, from the economic point of view, implementation of the B&R initiative will play a similar role as that Marshall Plan played in the process of European economic recovery and international integration.*

This quotation appears to be the discussion of "talking points" those Chinese public relations practitioners are urged to use when portraying the Belt and Road to Western journalists. Westerners have much to gain from eavesdropping upon what appears to be an "insider" conversation regarding how to Chinese public relations practitioners should present the Belt and Road to the larger world.

As anthropologists, Tian and Chen appear to be most at home when discussing the cultural aspects and implications of China's venturing into host communities. The authors affirm, "China should face up to many of its problems and restrictions." Doing so is a positive recognition of cultural distinctiveness and reflective of the authors' background as business anthropologists.

Although presenting views based upon the modern anthropological theory in Chapter 3, in Chapter 4, the discussions revert to Marxist rhetoric that seemingly reflects the point of view of Chinese leaders who are involved with the Belt and Road Initiative. Thus, the text observes:

> *Marx pointed out that the development of social and economic forms is a natural and historical process...[he] predicted that society would provide opportunities for people to display their creative abilities in an all-round way instead of limiting human development to a narrow range.*

Such phraseology and other representative examples of ideology that can be found, of course, venture into ideology and drift beyond scientific, academic writing. Such cases are useful to the reader because they demonstrate underlying premises held by members of the Chinese leadership who are involved with the Belt and Road initiative.

The ideological focus continues in Chapter 6, where the following observation is, once again, reflective of the Marxist thinking. Focusing upon conflict and dialectics, the text states:

> *The unjust and unreasonable international political and economic old order has not changed yet... In fact, at present, China has been entering an international friction period...this friction period will last for at least 20 years. This friction is not accidental but inevitable.*

Thus, China is establishing the Belt and Road initiative (a massive infrastructure project that is designed to increase its cultural and economic hegemony) during an era in which it believes inevitable international friction will dominate for at least the next 20 years. This is valuable information and the authors to be thanked for making it available to us.

In conclusion, the *Belt and Road vs. China and the World* provides a useful commentary regarding the Chinese Belt and Road Initiative. Although it might not be a genuinely academic treatise, it seemingly presents the Chinese point of view in a candid and straightforward to grasp manner. Understanding the prevailing Chinese perspectives regarding politics, ideology, and economics, as well as how they relate to the Belt and Road initiative, is very important. When reading with caution and from this perspective, the book has much to offer.

Acknowledgment

This work is deeply indebted to many Chinese scholars who did much to inspire it; we have referred hundreds of their articles and books published both in Chinese and in English. We thank Dr. Gao Jian, Dr. Jiang Youchun, Dr. Jiang Lifang, Dr. Li Rong, Liu Yu, Dr. Luo Kanglong, Dr. Ma Jianfu, Dr. Ma Zhanming, Dr. Shu Xiaohui, Dr. Wu Hexian, Dr. Xu Zonglin, Dr. Zhao Peihua, Dr. Zheng Muqiang, and Professors Le Guobing, Li Dekuan, Wang Tianjin, Yang Tingshuo, and Zhang Shaoping, for their insightful comments on and constructive suggestions to the initial manuscript, without their encouragements and supports this book may not be able to get published in time.

We thank our student Ms. Wang Ying who had participated in the project in the earlier stages and based on which we had published some articles in Chinese on the same topic. Our students, Mr. Ahsan Nawaz, Ms. Li Wei, Ms. Yu Hong, and Mr. Wan Yongan, helped our collected data and conducted some technique editing works. Ms. Ashley Yang, a professional translator, helped us translated considerable amounts of Chinese documents. Thanks also go to Dr. Russell Belk, Dr. Alf Walle, for their willingness to write the foreword for our book.

Finally, we would like to thank the Academic and Scholastic Publishing Foundations of Huaihua University and the Center for Social and Economic Behavior Studies of Yunnan University of Finance and Economics for their support to the publishing of this book.

Chapter 1
The Belt and Road Initiative

As a platform for international cooperation, the Belt and Road Initiative serves as a bond for peace with peaceful development and win-win cooperation as its principal target. Based on economic and trade collaboration, the Initiative also aims to promote political diplomacy and cultural exchanges. Construction of the Belt and Road Initiative is a demonstration of Chinese aesthetic value featured by openness, inclusiveness, peace and amicability. This chapter makes a comparative study on the Belt and Road Initiative and the Marshall Plan, which is launched by the United States for the revival of post-war Europe. It finds out that the two are intrinsically different in contexts, contents, and participants despite a few similarities.

Further, it analyses achievements and problems along the process as well as its impact on world strategic patterns. In all, the Belt and Road Initiative is a sign showing that Chinese opening-up has upgraded and entered a new phase of growth. It will, therefore, bring about a profound influence on the shared prosperity of the world. What is more, China should make a voice in cooperation when carrying out the Initiative. Also, China ought to propose cooperation between countries and regions that are conducive to world peace and strategic partnership featured by mutual help, benefits, and shared prosperity.

Introduction

The Belt and Road Initiative (from now on referred to as B&R, the Initiative, or the B&R Initiative) countersigns the contemporary development and realistic extension of the ancient maritime Silk Road. By borrowing from historical and cultural symbols of the old Silk Road, the initiative serves for multi-functions. Based on peaceful development and win-win cooperation, it considers economic and trade cooperation as the cornerstone, promoting political diplomacy and cultural exchanges to defuse potential risks. B&R, together with countries and regions along the line, aims to build the world's longest and most promising economic corridor that connects European civilization, Chinese civilization, Indian civilization, and Islamic civilization. At the same time, at this new historical moment, B&R construction highlights Chinese cultural values, such as being open, tolerant, peaceful, and friendly. And it is committed to building new cooperative relations with mutual benefits. With concerted efforts, China aims to come up with a community of shared interests in terms of politics, economic integration, cultural containment as well as sharing responsibility, destiny, and ecosystem, achieving Chinese Dream, Asian dream, a European dream, African Dream and the world dream (Fan and Zhang, 2016).

B&R is conducive to the promotion of world-wide interconnection. The Silk Road is a collective memory that embodies the spirit of peaceful cooperation in the history of interconnection. People of different regions, races, and cultural backgrounds miraculously created an arterial-like path linking politics, economics, culture, and ideology of the Chinese and Western world, just as torch relay. This road has never been a purely 'road' in a geographical sense, but an all-round and multidimensional network that includes road, trade, personnel exchanges, and culture exchange. B&R not only considers interconnection as the goal but also uses it as a driving path that can be treated as a methodological innovation. B&R is not in a hurry to formulate specific goals, rules, and plans, but is more process-oriented, concept-oriented and method-oriented. It attaches top importance to gradual and pragmatic cooperation and pays more attention to toughness and flexibility in the cooperation process. The methodology of interconnection seeks to establish a linking relationship between different countries and cultural systems, emphasizing that all parties should find an appropriate point for development strategy and bridge the thought and need for each country rather than using a necessary, hard-constraint uniform arrangement to require other participants (Su, 2016).

B&R leads to the new direction of global development. The latest round of globalization should place more emphasis on balance, linkage, and inclusiveness to ensure that world-wide event embodies better fairness and justice. B&R can lead the trend for the following reasons. First, B&R pays attention to infrastructure construction such as high-speed railways and energy pipelines so that it can promote the adjustment of global industrial layout. The Eurasian continent will gradually form a new economic network combining high-speed railways, expressways, energy pipelines, and electrical business logistics. It will derive progressively many new industrial chains, industrial bases, and economic centers. All the procedures mentioned above will change the economic landscape of the Eurasian continent, which will not only promote the development of the countries along the line but also benefit people, effectively reducing domestic and international inequalities. Second, B&R follows the idea of promoting cooperation and guaranteeing security through development. By deepening cooperation with countries along the line, B&R is dedicated to improving the development of the economy and people's livelihood, reducing poverty, and striving to eliminate terrorism and extremist. In this way, it actively contributes to the sound situation where mutual assistance between development and security can be found. Third, B&R is an open framework for international economic cooperation, which advocates the principle of openness and inclusiveness and embraces the participation of countries outside the boundary. It focuses on building bridges among international economic associations at various levels and in varying regions, resolving logical contradictions between globalization and global integration, and facilitating their mutual tolerance and mutual promotion.

As the platform for international cooperation, B&R serves as the bond of peace as well to happiness, both for China and the world as well. Despite difficulties in the process of construction, the pace of history will not stop. So, it will continue to overcome the challenges and seeks continuous improvement and development, displaying its unique advantages (Cui, 2017). In all, B&R will push the world forward from horizontal expansion to vertical deepening. The benefits of technology, industry, system, and mentality will be distributed more evenly across the globe. The balance and inclusiveness of the world's development will be further enhanced. And finally, B&R will benefit China as well as the world and facilitate a community of shared future (CSF) (Lin, 2017).

B&R Initiative and Its Influence on World Economic Structure

When delivering his speech at the 19th National Congress of the Communist Party of China, Xi Jinping pointed out that China adheres to the basic policy of opening-up, insists on engaging in construction with an open door, and actively promotes international cooperation underpinned by the B&R Initiative. During the process, China should endeavor to achieve connectivity and interconnection of policy, infrastructure, trade, finance, and people to create a new platform for international cooperation and add further impetus to joint development (Xi, 2017).

Also, the General Secretary of CPC Xi Jinping proposed to open fully and focus on B&R construction. Xi indicates that we should adhere to bringing in and going global and follow the principle of co-discussion, co-building, and co-sharing. While strengthening the ability for innovation and cooperation, we should put in place an efficient open pattern with a network covering land and sea, home and abroad, and East and West. We should also expand foreign trade, cultivate new trade models, and promote the ability of trading. We shall push business to an elevated level and adopt the free-and-convenient trading policy. The Pre-establishment of royal treatment and a negative list will protect the legitimate rights and interests of foreign investment and will also relax market access and expand the opening of the service industry.

Source: Orissapost (2017) Russia Wants India to Join OBOR Initiative. http://www.orissapost.com/russia-wants-india-to-join-obor-initiative/

Figure 1.1. Map showing areas under one belt one road initiative.

In his report, General Secretary Xi Jinping put forward that B&R construction is the succession of the Silk Road, keeping the latter's spirit of affinity, sincerity, benefit, and tolerance. B&R is different from Silk Road, but the former aims to activate the mind embedded in the Silk Road, such as peaceful cooperation, openness, and tolerance, mutual learning, and benefit. The broad sense of the Silk Road refers to the generic name of the line formed in ancient times (Wang, 2017). It was a line for long-distance commercial trade and cultural exchange covering Eurasia, North Africa, and East Africa. In terms of specific routes, it can be divided into the land Silk Road and the maritime Silk Road.

To spread Chinese culture and highlight national power, the ancient emperor sent envoys to all countries to open the land-and-sea Silk Road. It was Zhang Qian from Western Han Dynasty that went to the west for the second time when the well-known Silk Road was established. It also gained increasing popularity back then and saw the bustling scenes of visitors abroad calling at ports with people freely flowing (Li, 2017). Hundreds of years later, Ban Chao from the Eastern Han Dynasty went to the west again, which re-opened the land silk road from China to Eurasia.

The road started from the capital city Chang An and separated into two routes after passing the Hexi Corridor. One passes Yang Guan, Jin Shan-Shan, and moves to west along the north side of Kunlun Mountain.

Then it also gives Sha Che and Cong Ling before leaving Da Yue Zhi and heading south to Shen Du (today's India). Or it can pass An Xi (today's Iran) and Li Qian (today's Alexander of Egypt which was annexed by Roman in 30 B.C.). The second route passes Tulufan in Xinjiang providence after Yumenguan and heads to the west along the south road of Tian Mountain before passing Shu Le, Cong Ling (today's Pamir Region), Da Wan, Kang Ju and Yan Cai (north of Caspian Sea).

Later, with the decline of the land silk road, maritime Silk Road began to play an increasingly significant role in trades and served as the central passage for international exchanges. There are also two main routes in the maritime silk road, starting from the east sea or south sea. The east-sea way can be traced back to the beginning of the Zhou Dynasty (1046 B.C.) when Emperor Wu sent Qi Zi to North Korea to impart weaving techniques. Qi Zi set off from the Bohai Bay in the Shandong peninsula to reach North Korea. In this way, Chinese sericulture, silk reeling, and weaving techniques reached North Korea across the Huanghai Sea. After Tang and Song Dynasty, the South Sea became the central passage for international exchange, starting from Guangzhou, and so was named South Sea silk road. It came into being at Qin and Han Dynasty and grew up during the Sui Dynasty. Tang and Song Dynasty witnessed its blooming before declining at Ming and Qing Dynasty. It is the oldest sea route (Xiao, 2017).

B&R serves for multi-purposes: carrying forward Chinese culture, promoting economic development, and globalization. World-widely, developed countries begin to enter a new round of adjustment and upgrading of industrial structure: transferring large-scale industries to developing countries, accelerating modification and upgrade, increasing the level of industry transfer, and innovating the mode of industrial transmission. It indicates the overall transferring trend of the industrial chain. Synergic transfer of related industries had also increased. In addition, the dominant role of multinationals on mechanical adjustment and transmission is more prominent. The international industrial transfer provides a new opportunity to accelerate the upgrading of industrial structure, to realize industrial agglomeration, and to participate in the global division of labor. It also offers an opportunity for the adjustment of industrial structure and spatial distribution within the country.

The Belt and Road Initiative: Six Economic Corridors Spanning Asia, Europe and Africa

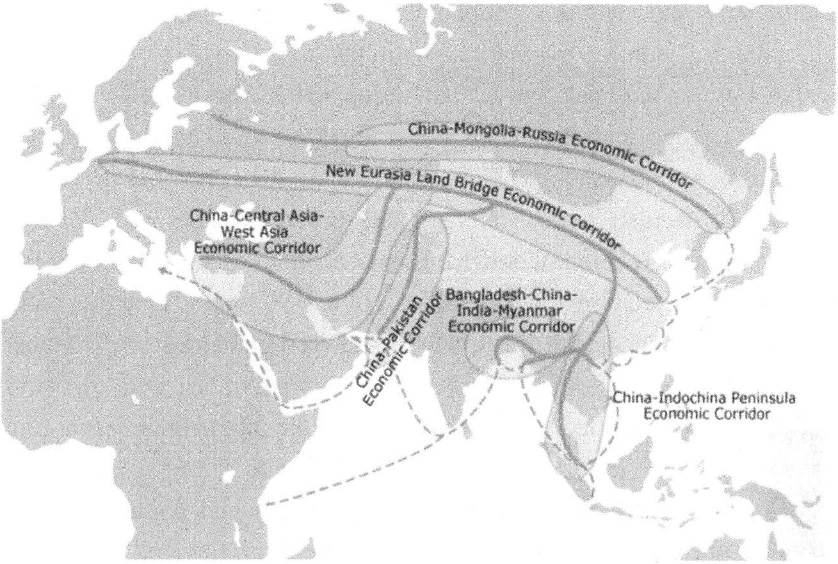

Source: HKTDC (2017) Interpreting the Belt and Road Initiative. HKTDC (Hong Kong Trade Development Council) Research, 268.

Figure 1.2. Economic corridors of one belt one road.

We are facing the opportunity of accelerating adjustment of industrial structure in various countries, which also coincides with the profound changes in ecological construction and economic growth pattern. The severe deterioration of the global ecological environment has forced states to set up environmental protection mechanism and change the way of economic growth. It can be foreseen that ecological protection and energy-saving industries will become an essential engine for future economic growth. It has become the consensus of the international community to develop a low-carbon economy and protect the ecological environment. The property of the clean energy industry will inevitably become the driving force for the new round of economic growth and influence the future of industrial development (Lin and Liu, 2017).

In recent years, the international political structure and trade rules have undergone significant changes. In the past, the global cooperation model with geographical proximity and similar cultural backgrounds were prevalent, such as NAFTA, ASEAN, and EU. Gradually, multilateral international cooperation, which is more flexible and cheaper, are gaining popularity. With the development of emerging economies, an international collaboration led by developed countries such as Europe and the USA has gradually shifted to the mode of multinational participation (Zhang and Deng, 2017). Global economic integration is also called international economic grouping. It is a product of both the internationalization of economics and the deepening of economic relations and interdependence between countries and regions. Its essence is to break administrative boundaries of divisions, plan layout, and organize specialized production and division cooperation in a unified manner according to the international economic principles. In this way, a consolidated market with shared interests and future can be built where members complement and collaborate. By reducing the transaction cost among member countries and increasing the freedom of trade, China will realize the free flow of elements and products and achieve the optimal allocation of resources. The essential feature of international economic integration is the alienation of sovereignty, voluntariness, and equality. They need to engage in an involuntary integration manner and enjoy equal rights in the institutions.

The construction of B&R has complied with the following trends: free trade agreement has become the mainstream of cooperation among countries; geographical space of economic integration expands continuously; the integrated organization is multi-layered and overlapping; institutionalized and standardized mechanism gradually come into being. It is beneficial to establish a unified market by China, Central Asia, and other countries along the Silk Road. They will maximize complementary advantages, cooperate, and form a community of shared interests to achieve shared prosperity.

New international relations advocate equity and justice, linking development on land and sea, reforming international order, and achieving inclusive globalization. In space, China must transcend the unfairness of the international law caused by the semi-globalization. Traditional globalization started from the sea. Coastal countries developed first while land-based countries and their inland areas are relatively backward, forming a massive gap between the rich and the poor. Because the oceans cover 71% of the earth and 90% of trade is carried out by the sea, the World Bank reported that 80% of global output comes from 100 kilometers of coastal areas. Then this kind of globalization can be called "semi-globalization." In terms of social attributes, the new international relations emphasize equality among big and small countries and build a community with a shared future. China should promote the evolution of the global system and make it fair and reasonable. B&R should overcome injustice caused by the big-bully-small logic. The traditional method was proposed by Europe, carried forward by the United States. So, it is west centered and leads to a series of adverse effects that the east follows the west; the rural areas belong to the city and the land affiliates to the sea.

B&R reflects China's good vision to seek peaceful development in the world. It surpasses the modern colonial system and the post-war hegemony system. The guiding idea of B&R resembles the Silk Road spirit: discussing together (brainstorming for a community of shared interests), building together (concerted efforts for a community of shared responsibilities), and sharing (joint beneficiaries for a community of shared future). They all lead to a new international relationship that embodies win-win cooperation.

General Secretary Xi Jinping pointed out in the report that we should insist on promoting the construction of the community of a shared future. Chinese dreams are interlinked with the goals of all peoples from all countries. The realization of the Chinese dream is inseparable from a peaceful international environment and a stable international order. China is unswervingly taking the path of peaceful development. We should pursue a mutually beneficial and win-win strategy of opening-up; we ought to uphold the right outlook and values; we should establish a universal, comprehensive, cooperative and sustainable new security concept; we had better seek an open, innovative, inclusive and mutually beneficial prospect; we shall promote civilized exchange and find common ground while reserving differences; we are obliged to build an ecological system that respects nature and braces green development. In all, we will always be a builder of world peace, a contributor to global growth, and a defender of the international order (Xi, 2017).

A Comparison between B&R and the Marshall Plan

B&R has become more explicit, and more corresponding measures are available. And then it is often compared with Marshall Plan which aims to revive Europe after postwar of U.S. The Chinese domestic media is more likely to believe that, from the economic point of view, implementation of the B&R initiative will play a similar role as that Marshall Plan played in the process of European economic recovery and international integration. Western scholars and media tend to form a political and security perspective and propose that B&R Initiative is the political security strategy of China to enlarge its influence and compete for international domination in the setting where the global power center has transferred. In fact, despite some standard features, B&R Initiative and the Marshall Plan are intrinsically different in backgrounds, contents, and participants.

Diverse Backgrounds

B&R Initiative is based on economic globalization and a multi-polarization world. In modern times, no country can only rely on its strength to achieve long-term and stable economic development. It is well known that the example of Boeing aircraft which are assembled on a global scale. The case perfectly proves that globalization is the current trend of economic development. After more than 30 years of reform and opening-up, today's China has accumulated a lot of excellent experience in manufacturing as well as abundant foreign exchange reserves. So, China is ready to go outside, given its qualifications and strength. In this case, the B&R Initiative is not only in line with the trend of this era, but also adequately reflects China's image as a significant and responsible power (Cheng, 2016).

In contrast, western European countries' economies slumped after the war. Besides, politics was left-leaning, and the influence of socialism rose. With obvious ideological purpose, the Marshall Plan aims to achieve dual control over Europe's economy and politics through conditional aid to Europe. It is planned to curb the influence of Soviet Socialists and consolidate established hegemonic positions of the United States. From the economic point of view, the pre-war economy of Europe that Marshall Plan aided was already well developed and enjoyed an elevated level of human capital. The trauma brought by the war destroyed the national infrastructure and led to temporary difficulties in economics (He and Xin, 2015).

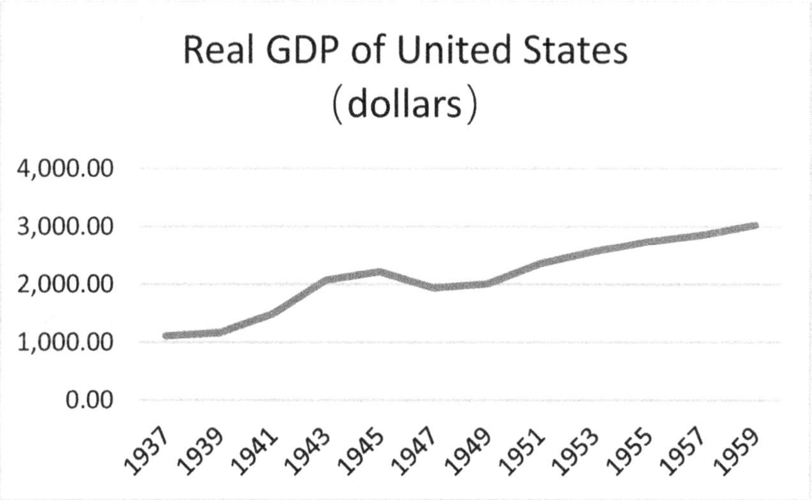

Fig 1.3 Real GDP of the United States

At the same time, the United States quickly entered the stage of overcapacity because the end of the war led to a rapid decline in the income from military munitions. What was more, the lowering power of European countries made it hard to purchase industrial products from the U.S., leading to an even worse economy (See Figure 1). In this case, to maintain 55 to 60 million people employed and to address the issue of growing overcapacity in the country, the United States started to implement the Marshall Plan since 1947. The plan had been in place for four years, and European countries had gained a lot of aid from the U.S., which brought substantial economic development. Europe's GNP rose from 119.6 billion dollars in 1947 to 158.8 billion dollars in 1951, increasing by 32.5%. At the same time, the output of industrial products in European countries also increased by about 40% compared with that in 1938. Agriculture increased by 10% (He and Xin, 2015).

In addition, the Marshall Plan aimed to compete with the Soviet Union for political-related rights after the war. Even Marshall himself said later that the final decision to give immediate assistance to Europe was made after the failure of the four foreign ministers' meeting in Moscow in 1947 (Tajovsky and Krcek, 2009). Marshall believed that the Soviet government had stalled and would not agree to any feasible plan to ease tensions and distress in Europe. Still, they would instead take every possible means to worsen the situation in Europe (Price, 1955).

Different Contents

On September 7th, 2013, when speaking at the Kazakh University of Kazakhstan, President Xi Jinping said that China was willing to cooperate with countries in Central Asia and innovatively build a "Silk Road Economic Belt." On October 3rd, 2013, when delivering a speech at the Indonesian Parliament, President Xi Jinping said that China was willing to strengthen maritime cooperation with ASEAN countries and work together for the construction of the 21st Century Maritime Silk Road. The building of the B&R Initiative is a strategy for joint development that aims at promoting exchanges between regions with an open and inclusive mentality. First, the B&R Initiative has strengthened strategic cooperation between China and relevant countries. The B&R Initiative aims to enhance the strategic partnership and mutual trust in politics between China and other countries along the line.

Second, The B&R Initiative aims to deepen China's energy cooperation with relevant countries, thereby to ensure energy security along the line and accelerating China's energy imports and exports. The "Silk Road Economic Belt" can strengthen the energy and economic ties between China and Central Asian countries. It also strives to promote diversified supply and sale channels of energy to ensure collective energy security for China and Central Asian countries (Zenn, 2015). Jacob Zeng, a scholar from the American Jamestown Foundation, believes that Gwadar Port in Pakistan ran by Chinese, shortens the distance between East Africa, Persian Gulf Port, and the west part of China, reducing 1/4 in comparison with Malacca Strait. Chiapas Bahr Port in Iran also has a similar function as Gwadar Port does. Elika Tangs from Jamestown Foundation believes that the B&R Initiative focuses more on excess domestic capacity instead of energy, and it looks for new markets abroad to help Chinese industries that had been hammered by slowing economic growth (Downs, 2015).

Third, B&R Initiative helps carry out cultural exchanges between China and other countries along the line. Through the Initiative, China aims to spread Chinese civilization and spread the Chinese Dream to the world. "Asia-Pacific Dream" is like a bridge that links the "Chinese Dream" and "World Dream," and B&R will also help its establishment. "Asia-Pacific Dream" keeps Asia Pacific Family Spirit and has a sense of destiny community. It leads the trend of world development towards a more peaceful and more productive life. In this sense, realizing the great rejuvenation of China synchronizes with achieving the "World Dream" for all humanity (Lu, Liu, and Yu, 2015).

In contrast, the Marshall Plan is a political and security strategy based on ideology with apparent exclusivity. Shouldering the strategic mission of stabilizing Europe to go up against the Soviet Union, the plan demonstrates the strategic intent of the United States to control Europe (Jin, 2015). Planners of the Marshall Plan feared that the Soviet Union could make use of the European crisis to expand further its influence, which may threaten U.S. security. Only the United States had enough economic power to restore the vitality of Europe and offer hope to the non-communist countries in Asia. If aid is not provided, escalating chaos will seriously endanger the free world and even threaten U.S. interests. Through U.S aid, the Marshall Plan had restored the European economy, making it a valuable tool to counter the Soviet Union. It also made it easier for the United States to occupy and control the European market. The Marshall Plan had harsh political conditions, and all the pro-Soviet countries in Europe were excluded. The United States set standards and rules to decide who could enter the program. Even allies and recipient countries can only accept unconditionally (He and Xin, 2015).

Different Participants

The B&R Initiative centers on countries along the ancient 'land Silk Road' and 'maritime Silk Road.' It also expands to other countries, including developing countries, emerging countries, and developed countries. By promoting economic cooperation and cultural exchanges between countries, it is keen on making effective use of complementary advantages of various countries, encouraging differentiated competition and economic integration. It also aims to create a new model for South-South cooperation, international cooperation, and intercontinental cooperation (Wang, 2015). The B&R is intrinsically an initiative or concept rather than a mechanism or an entity. The initiative is based on the principle of pragmatism and efficiency. By making full use of existing cooperation mechanisms, it innovates forms of cooperation according to the different priorities and conditions of the countries along the route, facilitating flexible development. The B&R Initiative does not seek to realize the leading power through a new system but is an advocate of pragmatic cooperation principle that respects local conditions and project orientation (Jin, 2015).

The Marshall plan, however, is the first group of countries' assistance offered to countries belonging to the second level. The participating countries include the United States, Britain, France, and other European capitalist countries. The socialist countries and the vast number of third-level countries are not involved. The Marshall Plan, through institutional arrangements and rules, seeks to dominate European affairs and maintain the supremacy of the United States. The importance of the aid is not its size, but its impact on European economic, fiscal, and monetary policies" (Price, 1955). To implement the Marshall Plan, the United States promoted the establishment of the 'European Organization for Economic Cooperation' in the first place. Although the principle of its establishment is "self-help and self-save," yet, as an observer and a backer, the United States made the organization an essential institutional tool to exert influence on European internal affairs. During the implementation of the Marshall Plan, the organization played a crucial role in analyzing the common economic difficulties and problems of the recipient countries, coordinating the policies of recipient countries, eliminating intra-European trade barriers, forming a multilateral payment system and establishing a European Payment alliance. Through the institutional role mentioned above, the United States made it possible for internal currency in Western Europe to convert freely. Then the U.S. dollar became a settlement currency between European countries. As a result, the U.S. dollar fixed its hegemony position, which changed the strict trade pattern among European countries and made the United States a dominant power after the war. By then, the new economic order was fixed (Jin, 2015).

Progress, Accomplishments, and Problems of the B&R Initiative

Learning from successful experience accumulated over the years, China carried out a strategic layout of the B&R Initiative: promoting the project from the top leaders, designing and implementing the framework, building the platform, and driving funds. With the promotion by China, the neighboring countries and other countries that are willing to take China's fast and passenger-friendly development express, and those international organizations that are embracing a better world economy, made various responses.

As a comprehensive means to serve China's opening-up strategy as well as a global strategy in the new era, there are already some achievements brought by the B&R Initiative in a brief time (Zhai, 2015). It does not mean, however, that there have no problems along the process.

President Xi Jinping stressed that to strengthen practical cooperation and actively promote the construction of the B&R Initiative. We should strive to find common interests of all parties and achieve mutual benefit. As outstanding support, the Asian Infrastructure Investment Bank has made substantial progress, such as the preparation of Silk Road Funds. China-Mongolia and China-Thailand Railways and other infrastructure are under construction and interconnected with each other. FTA negotiations between China and South Korea, China, and Australia have been making satisfactory progress (Wang, 2015).

From 2014 to 2016, China's global import and export trade totaled at 11.9 trillion U.S. dollars, with 6.7 trillion exportations and 5.2 trillion importations. During the same time, Chinese exportation to countries along the route was 1.8 trillion, taking up 27.4% of total Chinese exportation. As for imports, the number was 1.2 trillion, taking up 23.7% of the total importation. The proportion between China's exports to countries along the line and total Chinese exportation is enlarging every year. Trade surplus had also been increasing.

In 2016, China's foreign engineering contracting was 159.42 billion, increasing by 3.5% compared with last year. And new contracts' value was 244.01 billion, rising by 16.2% compared to the previous year. They both slowed down. While the turnover for the 61 countries involved in the Initiative was 75.97 billion, increasing by 9.7% and accounting 47.7% of the total, new contracting for the B&R Initiative was 126.03 billion, increasing by 36% and accounting 51.6% of the total contracting. In other words, increases of late and finished contracts for the B&R Initiative are higher than the overall growth. By the end of 2016, China established 56 economic and trade cooperation zones along the route, creating 177 thousand jobs for the local area. The total accumulated investment is more than 18.55 billion, and taxes paid to host countries by China is 1.07 billion (Xia, 2017).

When sharing with the globe about the B&R Initiative, the friendship between China and peoples of other countries has been widely promoted. Vigorous cultural exchanges and cooperation further connect people. By the end of 2016, China had signed a cooperation agreement on cultural exchanges with more than 60 countries along the road. In recent years, China has actively engaged in a full range of cultural exchanges with them, leading to a friendly atmosphere for cultural exchange.

The cultural exchanges and cooperation between China and other countries have ascended a new level since the birth of the initiative. In 2016, the 13th meeting of Cultural Ministers of SCO (Shanghai Cooperation Organization) member countries was held in Tashkent, the capital city of Uzbek. During that period, the Chinese Ministry of Culture sponsored the joint exhibition of the National Academy of Arts of China and Uzbekistan National Academy of Arts and Sciences; the Sino-Russian Cultural Forum has been held alternately since 2013. Cultural figures have been exchanging ideas in academics and thoughts to increase understanding of each other, which promotes a more in-depth communication and cooperation in various fields such as cultural policies, cultural mentalities, public cultural service, and cultural industry, etc. In April 2017, the Hungarian ballet Sissi staged in the Beijing Tianqiao Art Center, opening the curtain of the 17th annual Meet in Beijing festival. The festival is an excellent opportunity for Chinese people to know about Hungarian culture and is beneficial for cultural exchanges between the two countries. Also, China has established long-term cultural cooperation with Indonesia, Czech Republic, and other countries along the road, providing a platform and opportunity for more in-depth communication in the future (Wang et al., 2017).

According to the requirement of an all-round and deepening reform, government projects should be evaluated by professional departments and adjusted according to the evaluation results beforehand, during the process and afterward. For example, when B&R was launched in September 2013, domestic and foreign scholars proposed that the initiative might affect Russia's Eurasian Alliance Strategy. They advised the government to strengthen its communication with Russia. At the beginning of 2014, President Xi attended the Sochi Winter Olympics in person and talked with Putin about B&R. And after that, they reached a consensus on mutual support. Besides, the 'five-connection' policy, proposed by President Xi first in September 2013, refers to the connectivity of procedure, road, trade, currency, and people. In February 2015, it can be found both in Vice Premier Zhang Gaoli's speech and 'Vision and Action of the B&R Initiative' that 'road connection' is updated into infrastructure connection and the currency is changed into capital connection.

After adjustment, the two concepts are more encompassing and more realistic. Also, the content of the 'community of shared future' is growing in richness. It can be expressed as actively promoting the construction of the B&R Initiative and building a community of shared benefits, responsibility, and destiny. In this community, all members will trust each other in politics and work together with countries along the route for economic integration and cultural inclusion (Comprehensive Department of Ministry of Commerce of the People's Republic of China, 2015).

There are some achievements as well as problems in the process. Since 2014, Mr. Xi has made a few visits to Asian and African countries, spreading the B&R initiative and welcoming states along the border to share China's development opportunities to achieve shared prosperity (Xi, 2015). But it is not always plain sailing in the process of advancing, and there are still many problems. At present, the main issues are that people cannot reach a consensus on the nature of the initiative and have different opinions on its implementation.

First, in the Chinese domestic academic circles, there is 'generalization' and 'virtualization' when defining the B&R Initiative. Because of a wide range of areas involved in the initiative, scholars from different fields have identified an overall objective inclusive of all debatable issues in their area. Aim the B&R Initiative as an example; there are at least more than ten types of targets: to transfer excess capacity or promote international capacity cooperation; to push Chinese enterprises to go out; to open up overseas markets for Chinese enterprises; to get access to energy or resources from countries along the road; to promote the internationalization of RMB; to open up to the outside, especially to open up the inland area in of the Midwest of China; to pursue the strategy of economic diplomacy; to adopt a peripheral or global approach to serve China; to safeguard China's security in the west area; to reconstruct China's geo-political-and-economic strategy; to promote Chinese mode to the world; to promote China's participation in global governance and to expand its voice in it; to build a bridge of humanistic communication; to apply the geopolitical strategy of promoting rejuvenation of China, etc. Of course, the list can go on and on. Regardless of whether the Initiative alone, the capacity has to serve so many goals, attaching so many tags to it will cause fear and worry for the outside countries. A typical international challenge is that since these objectives are what China wants to achieve, why others are obliged to participate in and cooperate? Throughout global or international strategies launched by the world's major powers, there is never a single strategy that contains so many domestic goals. Of course, the Chinese do not deny the rationality of these objectives. And there is nothing wrong with linking them to the Initiative. However, the core matter is whether they can become strategic objectives of the B&R Initiative.

Second, the Initiative and local government's opportunism behavior might be related. One year after the Initiative was launched, by the end of 2014, the two sessions of the local governments were held. The Initiative was written into the development plan for all provinces and autonomous regions of the country. It is a positive signal indicating local governments' recognition and willingness to participate. But many local governments build infrastructures in the name of the Initiative, and the projects have a high degree of similarity. At the same time, many regions try to dig out their various silk roads in different dynasties to be listed as the central city or region to attract preferential policies of the central government. Many local governments regard the Initiative as an opportunity to solicit investment projects and preferential policies from the central government. In 2015, the central government issued The Belt and Road Initiative White Book, which cooled down this hot wave promptly and did not identify which cities were core cities (it only defined Xinjiang as the core of the land Silk Road and Fujian as the core of the maritime Silk Road). In recent years, this phenomenon has been curbed, but many decision-makers in local government have not eliminated their misunderstanding of the Initiative, and opportunism behavior still exists.

Third, some countries along the line consider the Initiative as China's foreign aid projects. Therefore, they are passive waiting and relying too much on China and sometimes raise a high price in cooperation. Since Chinese academics have given too many Chinese targets to the Initiative, some countries along the road see it as a foreign aid program launched by China to make itself an enormous power. For example, some states require the Chinese side to provide preferential interest rates to show bilateral friendship in some cooperative projects; they sometimes refuse to offer government guarantees for debt financing for infrastructure; they even proposed some business clauses that would make a loss for the investment, and so on. As a result, some projects had to be suspended. Besides, in Central Asia, influenced by traditional ideology, some people had an old impression on China, assuming that China is the same as during the period of Sino-Soviet confrontation. They maintain an elevated level of vigilance and precaution, thinking that the real intention of those Chinese companies who move there for development is to plunder their resources rather than help. This psychological prejudice and ideological gap on the Initiative created some risky uncertainty (Li, 2017).

Finally, among countries along the road, especially some big powers who are not involved, doubt about China's strategic motivation to promote the Initiative. On the one hand, scholars or officials in these countries are confused by confusing statements and explanation on the

Initiative by Chinese scholars and the media; on the other hand, they are in the state of hostility for China's growing up, and they have no faith in China's peaceful rise. This query has several types. Secondly, some regard the initiative as the Chinese version of the Marshall Plan. After the war, the United States carried out the Marshall Plan for the establishment of its hegemonic position in the world and made massive economic aid to its European allies. They compare the Initiative with the Marshall Plan and come up with the result that China is also planning to build its dominance. It is considered as China's hidden motivation to promote infrastructure, open up the market, and deal with excess capacity by western scholars. The real intention, in their opinion, is to achieve neo-colonialism through the Initiative. Thirdly, it revitalizes the tributary system. Holmes, an expert on Chinese issues at the U.S. Naval War Academy, points out that China is using economic favors in exchange for political obedience from its neighbor countries (Li, 2017). Because of these misunderstandings, the Initiative is interpreted as a type of national strategy of capitalism. In other words, it is regarded as an effort by a newly-emerging capitalist country to expand its sphere of capital with the help of national power (Wang and Li, 2017).

The Impact on the World's Economic Pattern

The economic and trade investment and international cooperation on capacity under the Initiative will implant new impetus into the development of the world economy. The Initiative will change the leading position of Europe and the United States in the global trading system. China, as the largest country of international business, is the biggest trading partner for 130 countries and regions in the world. Therefore, China can push forward optimizing and upgrading of doing business which is beneficial for more cooperation. China's investment in the Initiative will boost economic growth. With more than 3 trillion U.S. dollars as foreign exchange reserves, China has enough capital to invest in infrastructures related to the Initiative and meet requirements for industrial upgrading. These will help solve the bottleneck issues related to infrastructure in developing countries. At the same time, China cooperates with countries along the road in investment and production capacity, which can help developing countries achieve rapid growth (Chen and Tian, 2017).

As a national strategy of opening, the Initiative was proposed and carried out by China. It has efficiently promoted infrastructure construction for countries along the road and facilitates interconnection and trade growth. It also drives deeper South-South cooperation, which corresponds to the goal of joint development and an open, inclusive, and balanced world economy. It is, therefore, significant innovation and practical action of China to accelerate world economic growth inclusively and equitably as well as to reshape the world economic order (Xia, 2016).

In the context of the world's new standard economy, the world needs the Chinese economy to develop soundly. The Belt and Road Initiative is different from the mechanisms of cooperation in three aspects: openness, inclusiveness, and fairness. These three factors are precisely the essential elements in overcoming the difficulties in the trend of the world's new standard economy (Jia, 2017). Openness comes first. In the context of today's global order, the United States remains a significant provider of global public goods. However, in the face of a series of recent changes and trends, the existing international system cannot effectively keep up with changes in demand for global public goods. In the past, public goods are faced with high thresholds and must meet any additional conditions, so they cannot benefit developing countries. The initiative is based on the ancient Silk Road but is not limited to it.

Any country that accepts the cooperative concept of the Silk Road is welcome to participate. In terms of inclusiveness, the Initiative is not an entity or mechanism but is more like a concept or cooperation framework without any exclusion. Within this framework, there can be many cooperation mechanisms such as FTA, sub international cooperation, and economic corridor, which are based on a country's different political, economic, and cultural features. Hence, it will not replace or go against any international existing cooperation mechanism (Mao, 2015). The construction of infrastructure cannot be separated from the dedicated support of capital. According to predictions of the Asian Development Bank, there will be an investment need for 8 trillion dollars between the year 2010 to the year 2020. But from the perspective of existing global or international platforms for governance, most of the developmental financial institutions are less concerned about the list of developing countries. Existing multilateral financial institutions, such as the Asian Development Bank, provides only 10 billion dollars every year. The considerable funding gap severely restricts the overall development of developing countries (Wang and Xiang, 2015).

The B&R Initiative emphasizes on building an open, sharing, balanced, universal cooperation framework to break barriers between continents and sub-regions. So the global governance structure will develop continuously along an appropriate and reasonable direction, meeting the demands of developing countries: reshaping international economic and trade rules, reducing monopoly where few countries dominate in enactment and implementation of global economic and business regulations. It is China's exploration of optimizing global economic governance and building new international relations. And it is the contribution of China to promote mutual benefit in international cooperation and add more norms, openness, and justification to global economic governance.

The Initiative adheres to the concept of understanding, respecting, and sharing, aiming at building a world political structure featured by peace, harmony, and shared prosperity. Based on the global strategic point of view, the Initiative advocates the principle of equality and mutual benefit. When carrying out the strategy, China's influence on the world's political structure will be strengthened. The trend of globalization of core western countries is based on inequality, so the strategy of equality and mutual benefit mechanism will be resisted by the former (Ren, 2009). The conflicts caused by intrinsic differences of two devices will be felt in the way that core western countries will introduce a new mechanism to maintain the current status. China, however, will unite more developing countries in striving for a new order. In the process of strategy formulation, China takes full account of the political differences of various countries. In this way, China respects each other's will and helps establish a peaceful, harmonious, and common prosperous world legislative framework.

As a national development strategy featured by peace and win-win, the core of the Initiative is to promote balanced development of the region, to connect the sea and land trade corridors, and to build a green Asia-Europe economic circle. For international expansion, first, China should connect east and west areas within the country based on the achievements brought by China's Western Development Program and narrow differences between international development; second, China should expand coastal economic prosperity and enlarge advantage of the western area to achieve an around opening including inland-ocean and inland-inland pattern. For development strategy, China will share the benefits in the capital, technology, and equipment with countries all over the world and establish a global political and economic system which has sharing interests, responsibility destiny (Luo and Shi, 2017).

Post western international system and the modern global system have intrinsic differences, such as the decline of multi-polarization, globalization, and American hegemony (Li, 2002). Then, from a comparative perspective, there is a saying as the decline of the West and the rise of the East. Since the 1990s, there has been the trend of economic globalization and international collectivization world-wide. The IT-based technological revolution has led to a substantial growth of the global economy. From 1995, the World Trade Organization began to operate, and then economic groups such as the European Union, NAFTA and APEC started emerging. China overtaking Japan and becoming the world's second-largest economy, together with the rise of BRICS, trigger a reshuffle of the world economic structure. Jim O'Neill from Britain made predictions in a report titled 'Dreaming with BRICS: The Path to 2050' that by 2050, BRICS will surpass western developed countries including Britain, France, Italy and Germany, and will join the

United States and Japan as the world's six largest economies. In the post-western international system, international political power is moving eastward. The rise of the group of emerging powers represented by BRICS is a mark that the east is returning to the center of the international system. At the same time, this is also an indication that the world is moving towards a hegemony-free and balanced international order (Zhang, 2012).

Conclusion

The B&R Initiative marks a new stage of updating in China's opening and will produce a global dividend. President Xi Jinping pointed out that the Chinese cause is to cooperate with the world in a win-win manner. The international community is gradually becoming a community with a shared destiny. In the face of a complex world economy and global problems, no country can develop by itself. So it requires all states to work together as we are in the same boat. In other words, while pursuing our interests, China should also concern other countries and promote collective growth for all. In this way, China will build a more equitable and balanced new global partnership for development and create a better world. In terms of China's relationship with the world, the world needs a keen China, and China needs a peaceful and friendly world. To improve the Belt and Road Initiative, China should focus on building a new platform for cooperation, turning to a new impetus for growth, and exploring innovative ways of development. By working together for modern international relations with the core of win-win cooperation, we will enter a new phase of interconnection. All these will push the Initiative up along the ladder and facilitate world peace, harmony, and sustainable development.

In the second half part of the 20th century, peace and development became a universal theme. But after entering the new century, especially after 9.11, the idea was impacted by anti-terrorism, which made the international environment extremely complicated. Actions of western countries in recent years show that anti-terrorism work has a trend of expanding. What is more, there is a military layout on a global scale. It is a departure from the theme of peace and development. In this context, China must reaffirm the idea of peace and development at the right time. China should point out all deviating acts by political and military power to arouse moral judgments throughout the world. The implementation of the Initiative needs a peaceful environment as well as driving force motivated by demands and desires for development. If China can highlight the theme of peace and development, she will not only gain a good advantage but also can create a sound environment for the implementation of the Initiative.

After entering the 21st century, although factors that may cause the world's turbulence have not diminished nor have the economic and political relations between countries been significantly improved, yet in a sense, the concept of cooperation is possibly becoming a universal ideology. In this case, it is entirely possible to seek the right to boost collaboration. And if the Chinese can have a voice in cooperation, they will be able to solve many problems in international communication efficiently. As far as the Initiative is concerned, a partnership is embedded, but its essence has not explored in-depth enough. Therefore, for better carrying out the construction of B&R, it should be a priority to establish a Chinese voice during the cooperation. In this way, China should be able to put forward more beneficial advice to strengthen collaboration between countries and regions, to form a strategic partnership and to achieve mutual help and shared prosperity.

Besides Asian Investment Bank and the Silk Road Fund, China should expand its multi-channel sources of funding and enhance its fund-raising capabilities in the international market. For lowering loan risk, China can refer to the evaluation mechanism of existing international financial institutions. China can also supervise the entire process of lending and evaluate its future effect to ensure its maximum potential benefit can be achieved. For countries with abundant energy and natural resources but limited financial resources, China can design a flexible approach to offer loans in exchange for supplies. For innovative financial products, some measures can be made. In the first place, China can set up funds led by government equity, PPP guidance funds, and railway funds. Besides, China can also issue diverse types of securities, including Silk Road Bonds, to widen funding channels. What is more, China should establish a multi-input mechanism sponsored by the government and social capital.

China should set up a compensation fund to safeguard financial stability. At the same time, the mechanism for assistance for countries with financial risks should also be established to ensure financial security for countries along the route. Moreover, China should improve the insurance system for overseas investment. In detail, China should coordinate practical cooperation between policy-oriented insurance agencies and commercial-oriented ones, increase insurance aimed at foreign investment. Besides, China ought to set up a foreign investment fund, offering a guarantee for foreign investment to improve the strength and level of foreign investment insurance. Then in case of a state default, China Export and Credit Insurance Corporation will play its role as an escort: providing support against potential risk and offering a protective umbrella for Chinese overseas investment.

Chapter 2
Building Community of Human Destiny

Since been proposed by the Chinese President Xi Jinping in 2013, the "One Belt and One Road" major initiative has been highly concerned by the international community and has responded positively by the relevant countries, which has become a Chinese national strategy. The vision and action documents for the construction of "One Belt and One Road" have been formulated and written into relevant resolutions and records of the UN Security Council.

Introduction

The Chinese people focus on the construction of "One Belt and One Road" and adhere to the principle of "the combination of bringing in and going out." They abide by the policy of "constructing and sharing" and strengthen the opening and cooperation of innovative capabilities, to form an open pattern of linkage between lands, sea and abroad, which benefits both the east and the west. Up to now, the "One Belt and One Road" initiative has been actively responded to and participated in the world in the past five years. Noteworthy progress has been made in transforming the concept of "One Belt and One Road" from the vision to the real action. Compared with several significant plans in the history of world economic development, pushing forward the construction of "One Belt and One Road" has its characteristics and uniqueness. The goal of promoting the "One Belt and One Road" construction is to open wider to the outside world through expanding and further deepening reform, and to achieve mutual benefit and win-win cooperation with other developed and developing countries, and to build a community of human destiny.

The Belt and Road (abbreviated B&R) is the abbreviation of the "Silk Road Economic Belt" and "Marine Silk Road in the 21st Century."

In September and October 2013, Chinese President Xi Jinping put forward the cooperation proposal for building the new Silk Road Economic Belt and the Marine Silk Road in the 21st Century, respectively. On March 28, 2015, the State Development and Reform Commission, the Ministry of Foreign Affairs and the Ministry of Commerce jointly issued the "Vision and Action for Promoting the Construction of the Silk Road Economic Belt and the Marine Silk Road in the 21st Century."

Initial Accomplishments from the Construction of "One Belt and One Road"

About 2000 years ago, the hard-working and brave people of Eurasia explored many roads for trade and cultural exchanges that linked several significant civilizations in Asia, Europe, and Africa. These were collectively referred to as the Silk Road by later generations, which generally refer to the land silk road. It can be divided into land Silk Road and sea Silk Road. The land Silk Road originated in the Western Han Dynasty (202-8 BC) when Emperor Wudi of Han sent Zhang Qian to the Western Regions to open land corridors connecting the Mediterranean countries through Gansu, Xinjiang, Central Asia, and West Asia, starting from the capital Chang'an (now Xi'an). Its initial function was to transport silk produced in ancient China. In 1877, in his book China, the German geographer Richihofen named the "Silk Road" as "the western region transportation road between China and Central Asia, China and India through silk trade from 114 B.C. to 127 A.D.," which was quickly accepted and formally used by academia and the public. The "Maritime Silk Road" is a maritime passageway for ancient China's transportation, trade, and cultural exchanges with foreign countries. It is mainly centered on the South China Sea, so it is also called the South China Sea Silk Road. The Maritime Silk Road was formed in the Qin and Han Dynasties, developed from the Three Kingdoms to the Sui Dynasty, flourished in the Tang and Song Dynasties and transformed in the Ming and Qing Dynasties. It is the oldest known maritime route.

The proposal of "One Belt and One Road" initiative

For thousands of years, the spirit of peaceful cooperation, openness and tolerance, mutual learning, mutual benefit, and win-win of the Silk Road has been handed down and promoted the progress of human civilization. It is a vital link to promote the prosperity and development of countries along the Silk Road, an important symbol of East-West exchanges and cooperation, and a famous historic and cultural heritage shared by all countries in the world. In the 21st century, in the new era with the theme of peace, development, cooperation and win-win situation, facing the complicated international and regional situation, it is more important and precious to inherit and carry forward the spirit of the Silk Road. In September and October 2013, during the visit to Central Asian and Southeast Asian countries, Chinese President Xi Jinping put forward a significant proposal to build the "Silk Road Economic Belt" and "the maritime Silk Road in the twenty-first Century" (referred to as the "One Belt and One Road") successively, which is highly concerned by the international community and gains a positive response from the states.

Speeding up the construction of "One Belt and One Road" is conducive to promoting economic prosperity and regional economic cooperation among various countries along the road, strengthening exchanges and mutual learning among different civilizations, and promoting world peace and development. It is a prime cause for the benefit of people from all over the world. The strategy of building the "One Belt and One Road" strategy has become China's national strategy and has been actively responded by the relevant countries along the way and has won widespread resonance. On November 4, 2014, Xi Jinping chaired the eighth meeting of the Central Leading Group on Finance and Economics. It delivered a critical speech emphasizing that the Silk Road Economic Belt and the 21st Century Maritime Silk Road Initiative conformed to the requirements of the times and the aspirations of all countries to accelerate development. It provided an inclusive and huge development platform with a profound historical origin and humanistic foundation and could equate the rapid growth of China's economy with that of other countries. He also pointed that the nation should concentrate its efforts on this significant event, uphold the concept of neighboring diplomacy of kindness, sincerity, beneficence, and tolerance, and have harmonious relations with nearby and distant states, to make the countries along the road more identify with China and become closer and more supportive.

On March 28th, 2015, President Xi Jinping delivered a keynote speech at the opening ceremony of the Boao Forum for Asia in 2015, saying that the "One Belt and One Road" Cooperation Initiative fits the needs of China, the countries along the border and the region, meeting the common interests of all the parties concerned, and complying with the trend of regional and global cooperation. The construction of "One Belt and One Road" is based on the principle of collaboration, co-construction, and sharing. It is not closed but open and inclusive. It is not a solo of the Chinese family, but a chorus of the countries along the route. The construction of "One Belt and One Road" is not to replace the existing regional cooperation mechanisms and initiatives, but rather to push the development strategies of the countries along the border to complement each other and help with each other's shortcomings. With the joint efforts of all parties concerned, the vision and action document for the construction of "One Belt and One Road" has been formulated.

The infrastructure investment bank of Asia has made substantial progress in its preparation and construction. The Silk Road Fund has successfully started, and several infrastructure interconnection projects have been steadily advancing. On March 28, 2015, the Chinese Government officially announced the Vision and Action for Promoting the Co-construction of the Silk Road Economic Belt and the Marine Silk Road in the 21st Century (from now on referred to as "Vision and Action"). "Vision and Action" put forward five valuable contents and cooperation priorities: policy communication, facilities interconnection, trade flowing, accommodation of fund, and the same hearts and minds among people. The Thirteenth Five Year (2016-2020 year) Planning Outline for People's Republic of China's National Economic and Social

Development, issued on March 17, 2016, pointed out: the nation should improve the "One Belt and One Road" cooperation mechanism, and improve the "One Belt and One Road" bilateral and multilateral cooperation mechanism around policy communication, facilities interconnection, trade flowing, accommodation of fund and the same hearts and minds among people so that the states can create a new situation of open and inclusive human exchange. Besides, the nation should build a mechanism for cultural transactions involving both officials and citizens.

On August 17th, 2016, President Xi Jinping delivered a speech at the Forum of "One Belt and One Road" to push forward and to promote the construction work of "One Belt and One Road" by reviewing the historical experience and previewing the future outcomes. He stressed the importance of summarizing experience, strengthening confidence and advancing steadily. He indicated that the nation must focus on policy communication, facilities interconnection, trade flow, and financing and common people's hearts. He insisted on focusing on building a mutually beneficial cooperation network, new cooperation mode and multi cooperation platform, focusing on building green silk together. One belt, one road, is to bring along the "one belt" road to the people of all countries along the route.

Xi Jinping pointed out that there were more than 100 countries and international organizations involved in the project. China signed a cooperation agreement with more than 30 countries along the route to carry out the "One Belt and One Road" cooperation agreement and international capacity cooperation with more than 20 countries. International organizations, such as the United Nations, also took an active attitude. Financial assistance, represented by the Asian Investment Bank and the Silk Road Fund, has been deepening, and a few essential landmark projects have gradually landed. The construction of "One Belt and One Road" is from scratch to existence, from a point to the surface, with progress and achievements exceeding expectations.

On March 18th, 2017, the UN Security Council resolution called on all countries to promote the construction of "One Belt and One Road" and build a community of human destiny. The Resolution No. 2344th on Afghanistan unanimously adopted by the UN Security Council[1], called on the international community to condense the assistance of the Afghan consensus and strengthen regional economic cooperation through the construction of "One Belt and One Road," urging all the parties to provide a safe environment for the "One Belt and One Road" creation to strengthen the strategic docking of development policies and promote interoperability and pragmatic cooperation. The resolution emphasizes that regional cooperation should be supported in a spirit of win-win cooperation to effectively help security, stability, and development in Afghanistan and the region and build a community of human destiny. So far, the construction of "One Belt and One Road" has been officially written into the United Nations documents.

Initial Outcomes of "One Belt and One Road" Construction

On May 14th, 2017, Xi Jinping delivered a speech at the opening ceremony of the International Cooperation Summit on the One Belt and One Road[2], in which Xi addressed that more than 2000 years ago, the Chinese ancestors crossed the prairie desert and opened the land Silk Road connecting Asia, Europe, and Africa. The Chinese forefathers set sail and sailed through the stormy waves to break out the Silk Road on the sea connecting East and West. The ancient Silk Road opened a new window for friendly exchanges among countries and wrote a new chapter in human development and progress. The old Silk Road stretches for thousands of miles and lasts for thousands of years. It has accumulated the spirit of Silk Road with peace and cooperation, openness and tolerance, mutual learning, and mutual benefit as its core. It is the precious heritage of human civilization. The Chinese people believe that this period of history shows that no matter how far apart they are if they bravely take the first step and persist in moving towards each other, they can walk out of the road of meeting and knowing each other with typical development and happiness, peace, harmony, and beauty.

In the autumn of 2013, President Xi proposed the construction of the Silk Road Economic Belt and the maritime Silk Road in the twenty-first Century in Kazakhstan and Indonesia, that is, the "One Belt and One Road" initiative. Peach trees are not attractive, but because they have flowers and fruits, people walk under them and make a path. Similarly, being noble, honest, and upright will naturally be respected and admired by people without self-declaration. Over the past four years, more than 100 countries and international organizations in the world have actively supported and participated in the construction of "One Belt and One Road." It has also been included in the relevant resolutions of the UN General Assembly and the UN Security Council. The construction of "One Belt and One Road" has gradually transformed from a concept into action, from vision to reality with fruitful progress. President Xi has said many times that the construction of "One Belt and One Road" is not to start a new business or reinvent the wheel but is to achieve strategic docking and complementary advantages among states along the road. The Chinese coordinate their policies with relevant countries, including the Eurasian Economic Union proposed by Russia, the Master Plan for Interconnection offered by ASEAN, the "Bright Road" proposed by Kazakhstan, the "Intermediate Corridor" proposed by Turkey, the "Road of Development" submitted by Mongolia, the "Two Corridors and One Circle" proposed by Vietnam, the "North Economic Center of England" offered by Britain, the "Amber Road" submitted by Poland, and so forth. Planning docking between China and Laos, Cambodia, Myanmar, and Hungary have also been carried out in an all-round way.

It has been several years since the people's hearts and minds have been united. The friendship between the nation and the people lies in the heart-to-heart relationship. The construction of "One Belt and One Road" has helped the participating countries to carry forward the spirit of the Silk Road, carry out the structure of the intelligent Silk Road and the healthy Silk Road, and extensively cooperate in various fields such as science, education, culture, health, and folk exchanges with each other, to lay a solid foundation for the "One Belt and One Road" construction and build a solid foundation for the society. The fruitful results show that the “One Belt and One Road” initiative is in line with the trend of the times and meets the laws of development. It is also in line with the interests of all peoples and has broad prospects.

Xi stressed that China should build the “One Belt and One Road” into the road of civilization. The “One Belt and One Road” initiative aims to transcend estrangement among cultures, promote mutual learning among civilizations, transcend conflict among civilizations, and advance coexistence among civilizations beyond their superiority. It seeks to promote mutual understanding, mutual respect, and mutual trust among countries. The construction of “One Belt and One Road” is rooted in the historical soil of the Silk Road, focusing on the Eurasian continent and opening to all friends. Whether from Asia, Europe, Africa, or America, all states are partners in building international cooperation with the “One Belt and One Road.” The construction of “One Belt and One Road” will be discussed by all of us, and the achievements of the “One Belt and One Road” construction will be shared by all as well.

The ancient Silk Road embodies the pursuit of a better life of our ancestors, promotes the interconnection of countries in Asia and Europe, promotes the exchange of civilizations between the East and the West, and makes significant contributions to the development and progress of human culture. The Chinese believe that they can absorb wisdom and strength from the ancient Silk Road, promote cooperation in the spirit of peaceful cooperation, openness and tolerance, mutual learning and mutual benefit and win-win situation, and jointly open a brighter future. “One Belt and One Road” originated from China but belonged to the world. The construction of “One Belt and One Road” is an open and inclusive cooperation platform spanning different regions, various stages of development, and different civilizations. It is a global public product jointly built by all parties. It focuses on the Eurasian continent and is open to all like-minded friends, without excluding or targeting either side.

China’s efforts to promote “One Belt and One Road” construction should strengthen international cooperation, economic policy coordination, and development strategy docking, transform consensus into action, and develop practical cooperation in various fields, and continue to reach new achievements, set up bridges for non-governmental exchanges and create better lives for the people. All countries are equal participants, contributors, and beneficiaries in promoting such an open and inclusive development platform of "One Belt and One Road" construction. With an open mind, China will adhere to the principles of consultation, joint contribution and sharing, mutual respect, democratic deliberation, and collective decision-making, and work together in the opening and win-win cooperation.

On October 18, 2017, the report of the Nineteenth National Congress of the Party pointed out that the nation should promote the formation of a new pattern of large opening up. We should focus on the construction of "One Belt and One Road," adhering to the principle of "the combination of bringing in and going out," abiding by the policy of "joint contribution and sharing," and strengthening the opening and cooperation of innovative capabilities, to form an open pattern of linkage between land, sea and abroad which benefits both the east and the west. Up to the current time, the "One Belt and One Road" initiative has been actively responded to and participated in the world in the past five years. After five years of practice, the "One Belt and One Road" construction has made considerable progress from the concept and vision to practical action.

First, enhance strategic mutual trust and build up international consensus. The core idea of building the "One Belt and One Road" initiative and co-building and sharing have been written into the outcome document of important international mechanisms such as the United Nations. One hundred and three countries and international organizations have signed 118 cooperation agreements with China on "One Belt and One Road." In 2017, the first "One Belt and One Road" International Cooperation summit was successfully held in Beijing. The heads of state and government of 29 countries attended, and 1600 representatives from more than 140 countries and more than 80 international organizations participated in the meeting. Of the 279 outcomes of the Forum, 265 have been completed or turned into regular work so far, and the remaining 14 are being supervised and promoted, with the implementation rate reaching 95%.

Second, pay close attention to cooperative projects and form demonstration effects. Focus on the main framework of "Six Corridors, Six Roads, Multi-Countries and Multi-Ports," substantive progress has been achieved in several cooperation projects. The construction of the China-Pakistan economic corridor is progressing smoothly. The creation of China-Laos, China-Thailand, and Hungary railways has steadily advanced. Some sections of the Yawan high-speed railway have been constructed, and Guadall Port has been equipped with full operational capacity. On August 26, the cumulative number of block trains in China and Europe exceeded 10,000, reaching 43 cities in 15 European countries, reaching the achievement of "three trips of going and two trips coming back," with a substantial box rate of 85%.

Third, promote win-win cooperation and achieve joint development. As of June 2018, China's trade in goods with countries along the route totaled more than $5 trillion, and the foreign direct investment exceeded $70 billion. Overseas Economic and trade cooperation zones built by countries along the line have invested more than 20 billion US dollars, created hundreds of thousands of jobs, and generated billions of US dollars in tax revenue for local governments. At present, Chinese enterprises have been exploring with companies in the developed countries, including some large multinational companies to build the third-party market cooperation in the "One Belt and One Road" construction field.

Fourth, improve the service system and strengthen financial support. China and 17 countries have approved the "One Belt and One Road" financing guidance principle, accelerating the overseas layout of financial institutions, and 11 Chinese funded banks have set up 71 first-tier institutions. Joint financing cooperation with multilateral development banks such as the African Development Bank, the Pan-American Development Bank, and the European Bank for Reconstruction and Development, has been carried out. The Chinese should strengthen legal risk prevention and control and initiate the establishment of the "One Belt and One Road" international commercial dispute settlement mechanism and institution.

Fifth, uphold openness, tolerance, and enhance cultural exchanges. The states should actively carry out cooperation in education, science and technology, culture and other fields, and formulate and publish special cooperation plan education, science and technology, finance, energy, agriculture, inspection and quarantine, standard Unicom and other areas. Through the implementation of the Silk Road Scholarship Scheme and the establishment of school-running institutions abroad, technical management talents will be cultivated for the countries along the Silk Road. In 2017, there are more than 300,000 students came from countries along the line to China, and more than 60,000 students went out to countries along the route. It is estimated that by 2020, the number of two-way tourists with countries along the line will exceed 85 million, and tourism consumption will be about 110 billion US dollars.

Several Major Plans in the World Economic Development History

White Plan

In July 1944, on the eve of the victory of World War II, 44 allies in World War II, organized by the United Kingdom and the United States, held a 730-member International Monetary and Financial Conference of Union and Alliance Countries at a hotel in Bretton Woods Village, New Hampshire, USA, and adopted the International Monetary Fund Association and the International Bank for Reconstruction and Development Agreement based on the White Plan proposed by the United States, also known as the Renault Plan. They were finally recognized as the Bretton Woods Agreement[3], marking the start of the Bretton Woods System. In the international financial and monetary system, the US dollar is the unified unit of currency settlement in the world (Zhou, 1984).

First, since the implementation of the Bretton Woods Agreement, US dollar bonds have become the world settlement currency, dominated the world financial and monetary market, and the US dollar allows the United States to borrow from the world without restriction. Still, its debt repayment is unequal or merely irresponsible. Besides, since the U.S. debt to other countries is denominated in U.S. dollars, it can allow money printing mills to overprint the U.S. dollar without restraint. In such cases, even if the dollar depreciates, it can reduce the burden of their external debt, stimulating exports, and improving their balance of payments (Ding, 2011).

Besides, with the muscular economic strength and stable investment environment of the United States, investment and financing in the United States can bring more profits. Therefore, many people and many countries want to invest and finance in the United States. For this reason, the arrival of many circulating dollar funds has reduced its interest rate and reduced the cost of making up the fiscal deficit. Moreover, under normal circumstances, when a country's balance of payments deficit occurs, it is generally necessary for the government to adjust its economic policy. Still, the United States does not need to do so because the United States dollar is an international currency. When the United States has a foreign trade deficit, the United States government can print U.S. dollars to offset the deficit, maintaining the balance of the national economy, and transferring inflation to other countries (Xu, 2006). This is the main reason why the post-war U.S. economy remains stable despite decades of high fiscal deficits for decades.

Moreover, in the world economic risk, the United States can also obtain a colossal Seigniorage tax, which was initially being imposed by Western European countries in the Middle Ages on precious metals such as gold and silver sent to mints for coinage. Later, the profits made by the U.S. government in issuing currency (equal to the difference between the face value of coins and the value of coin metal coins) were based on paper money after the collapse of the gold standard. The paper-based credit standard replaced the gold standard, and the US dollar acted as the international monetary agent, which brought great benefits to the United States (Zhao, 1980). When the United States prints a worthless note bond, the Seigniorage is equal to the value of the social products it can buy. The difference between them is the "Seigniorage tax" of the United States. Such a dominant position in the world economic and monetary rate has brought significant economic benefits to the United States.

Why can the Bretton Woods Agreement be implemented smoothly? At the end of World War II, Italy had surrendered, Germany had turned to strategic defense on the eastern front, and Japan had lost its ability to conduct large-scale battles in the Pacific region. Not only the domestic economy of these three countries was close to collapse, but also the economic strength of Britain and France had been severely damaged in the war. At that time, the war economy of the Soviet Union was the same as that of Britain and France as Fascist Nazi Germany invaded it before the completion of its third five-year plan. It was only the United States that made windfall profits in the war. As a result, its economy developed unprecedentedly, and gold flowed into the United States continuously. In 1945, the gross national product of the United States accounted for 60% of the total domestic production of the capitalist countries. The gold reserve of the United States increased from $14.51 billion in 1938 to $20.8 billion in 1945, accounting for 59% of the world's gold reserve, equivalent to 3/4 of the world's gold reserve of the whole capitalist society, which made it a dominant position in the capitalist world. Therefore, in the wartime era of the world economy under this situation, it was necessary to form an international monetary system centered on the US dollar after World War II.

In addition, according to the announcement of the National Security Agency in 1994, the circulation of US dollar bills worldwide is 400 billion dollars, 1/3 of which is in the United States and the other 2/3 in foreign countries. The New York Federal Reserve also reported that, at the end of 2002, about 55% to 60% of the $650 billion currencies circulated on the market, or about $340 billion to $370 billion, was distributed outside the United States. According to recent estimates of the Federal Reserve System, about two-thirds of all currencies are held outside the United States, and the total amount of currencies circulated the world has reached nearly $70 billion. Between 1989 and March 1996 alone, US dollars flowed to Russia and Argentina amounted to 44 billion and 35 billion US dollars, respectively. The material and labor costs of printing a US dollar bill were only US$0.03, which, however, could buy goods worth the US $1. As a result, the US received huge Seigniorage revenue of more than US$30 billion annually, and the cumulative income since World War II was about US$3 trillion.

According to the last data of the Federal Reserve, the total amount of M3 dollars is about 103 trillion US dollars, and it is impossible to determine the accurate statistical data for many reasons. For example, in addition to private collection and banking, it is always difficult to count the lost and destroyed U.S. dollars collected by people. With a long history, U.S. dollars (except Lincoln Green Currency) can be used in circulation in all periods. As long as the Federal Reserve does not fail, any dollar that can be certified can be effectively utilized and circulated with value and purchasing power. There is no problem with invalid currency because the Federal Reserve is independent of the government and is an unusual and weird financial institution system.

Marshall Plan

The Marshall Plan, which is officially known as the European Recovery Program, was a plan carried out by the United States after World War II to offer economic assistance and reconstruction for the war-torn Western European countries, which had a far-reaching impact on the development of European countries and the world political pattern. The plan was officially launched in July 1947 and lasted for four fiscal years. During this period, by participating in the European Economic Cooperation Organization (OEED), Western European countries received a total of 13.15 billion US dollars in various forms of assistance, including finance, technology, and equipment, 90% of which were grants and 10% were loans.

The "European Renaissance Plan" was formulated by the United States after the end of World War II to provide economic assistance for the reconstruction of war-torn Western European countries, which had a far-reaching impact on the development of European countries and the construction of the world economy. The Marshall Plan was officially launched in July 1947 and lasted for four fiscal years. During this period, by participating in the European Economic Cooperation Organization (OEED), western European countries accepted various forms of assistance and cooperation from the United States in finance, technology, and equipment, totaling 13.15 billion US dollars, 90% of which were gifts and 10% were loans (Lin, 2017).

Six years after the end of the war, most of Europe was still unable to recover from the deaths and injuries of hundreds of millions of people. The battle spread all over the continent, covering a much larger area than the First World War. The continuing bombing had severely damaged most cities, such as Warsaw and Berlin, which had become a ruin, especially their industrial production. London and Rotterdam had been severely damaged. Most of the economic output and related buildings in these countries and regions had been reduced to rubble. Agricultural destruction had led to widespread hunger in many parts of the European continent. At the same time, the rare winter in Northwest Europe from 1946 to 1947 made this situation worse. Hundreds of millions of people were homeless. The most severe problem was transportation facilities of which railways, bridges, and roads were the targets of air raids during the war, and merchant ships for transportation were often sunk. It took a lot of money to solve these problems. At this moment, the treasuries of most countries in the war had been exhausted, resulting in economic instability and the global economic downturn. Under this situation, the United States had experienced isolationism and tried to promote the growth of the European economy.

Through the U.S. Congress bill, several major banks were decided to implement the "Marshall Plan," referring that the United States intervened in other countries' political, and economical construction by increasing the number of loans to other countries, and directed these debts directly to the unpaid "Marshall Plan." So far, the "Marshall Plan" still shows its hegemonic power of the United States. Another crucial factor is that at the beginning of the cold war, the suspicion of the Soviet Union's actions in the United States was deepening. At that time, George Kennan, one of the advocates of the Marshall Plan, put forward his new theory of the political polarization pattern in the future world to support the Marshall Plan. He pointed out that the core content of the Soviet Union's containment policy would be effectively carried out. What needs to be emphasized is that when the "Marshall Plan" began to be implemented, the cold war between the Soviet Union and the United States began to flourish, during which the fear of the Soviet Union even overrides international political factors. But in fact, American policymakers did seriously consider this possibility and realized the disintegration of the Soviet Union, which served to curb Russia's economic development and expansion, but failed because, at that time, Europe still hoped that the Soviet Union would join the "Marshall Plan." Hence, the Soviet Union was, at last, separated from the "Marshall Plan" successfully (Milesheimer, 2017).

Before the implementation of the Marshall Plan, the United States had invested tens of billions of dollars in European reconstruction, including financial leasing, indirect lending, infrastructure lending, and business loans and assistance, as well as multilateral trade and bilateral cooperation, which covered military bases, weapons, and equipment. In July 1947, at the Marshall Plan Conference which was widely attended by European countries, the Organization for Economic Cooperation and Development (OECD) in which Western European countries participated received a total of 13 billion U.S. aid in various forms, including finance, technology, and equipment, which was equivalent to 130 billion U.S. dollars in 2006.

On the one hand, the "Marshall Plan" initially considered cooperation with the Soviet Union on the condition that the Soviet Union had to carry out political reforms. Still, the Soviet Union did not agree to it. On the other hand, the United States feared that the Soviet Union would use the "Marshall Plan" to restore and develop its strength, so the United States and Western countries put forward many harsh terms that the Soviet Union could not accept, leading to the result that the Soviet Union eventually was excluded from the "Marshall Plan." When the Marshall Plan came to an end, the national economy of most of the Western European countries except East Germany had recovered to its pre-war level. In the next 30 years, the whole Western European economy experienced an unprecedented period of rapid development, and the social economy showed a prosperous picture. It can be said that the Marshall Plan is closely related and that it is one of the key factors contributing to European integration. Even when the "Marshall Plan" was eliminated or weakened, the economic ties of the Western European countries became closer and closer, eventually leading to an integrated economy. The Marshall Plan has systematically learned and adapted to the experience of the United States in the economic management of Western European countries.

Under all these circumstances, the Marshall Plan is a plan designed to help the United States recover from the destruction of its economy caused by the war in the European Union because of World War II and to curb the further expansion of Communist forces in Europe. Therefore, the official claimed that the "European Recovery Plan" (ERP) is wholly implemented. Its main sponsor was then US Secretary of State George Marshall, but many officials of the US State Department, especially William Clayton and George Kennan, designed the plan. When Ernest Bevan, then British Foreign Secretary, heard of the Marshall Plan, he immediately contacted George Beedo, then French Foreign Minister. They exchanged views of the European side on the assistance provided by the United States to Europe. At the same time, the two foreign ministers agreed that it was necessary to invite the Soviet Union, an essential ally of the anti-fascist war, to participate in the European Renaissance Plan (ERP). If this happened, the Soviet Union would be frankly welcomed to join in the "European Recovery Plan" to receive assistance from the United States. However, Stalin could not agree to participate in the "Marshall Plan" because he believed that the Soviet

Union was in a very favorable international environment after the war, so ultimately the Soviet Union rejected the "Marshall Plan" (Bi, 1992).

The Marshall Plan came to an end in 1951. Since then, Western Europe has begun an unprecedented development for 30 years. Today, people generally believe that the "Marshall Plan" accelerated the development of the Western European economy, but it did not start the economic take-off of Europe. From the political and economic influences, the implementation of the Marshall Plan freed Western Europe from the financial constraints in the early post-war period, and the situation of limited rationing caused by material shortages reduced people's dissatisfaction with the government and stabilized the political situation. Although some countries' regime supported the United States at first, its political action has aroused strong resentment among many nations. Notably, the world economic development prospects today have made more countries and people become disgusted and opposed to the US trade negotiations. To this end, China's "one belt and one road" initiative is the development prospect of the destiny community of human beings and is a mutual benefit and win-win of humanitarianism and civilization construction in the development of the social economy.

The "one belt and one road" construction plan

To the Chinese people, promoting the "One Belt and One Road" construction is fundamentally different from the Marshall plan. In the past years, since the "One Belt and One Road" initiative has been put forward, some scholars mistook the initiative of "One Belt and One Road" with the post-war revival of the European "Marshall plan." Western scholars and media reported that they scored from the perspective of politics, economy, and security, holding the opinion that the implementation of the "One Belt and One Road" initiative has a similar function with the "Marshall Plan," which played the same role in the European economic recovery and regional integration process. For this reason, the US and the western power factions think it is not suitable to carry out the construction of China's "One Belt and One Road," taking the excuse that it is a dictatorial act. To prevent the development of "One Belt and One Road," the U, S. government-imposed trade frictions on the Chinese government at all costs and carried out international trade wars from political economy to trade negotiations, from financial marketplace to global policies, making this peace square of the world a new world pattern of economic development full of tense (Ming, 2015). To this end, the transfer and mechanical adjustment of international industrial-economic centers are based on mutual respect, in line with their respective interests and political backgrounds. The mode of worldwide production and world economic development means to compete for dominant power and regional cooperation within the scope of economic forces and to seek plans in the strategic development of political security.

The Marshall plan and the "One Belt and One Road" are fundamentally different from each other in terms of their background, content, times, and leading participants. As the construction of "One Belt and One Road" needs to take the experience of world economic globalization and world diversification into account, no country can rely on its strength to achieve long-term economic stability and development. We all know that Boeing planes are manufactured globally and assembled in Boeing's factories, which proves that globalization is the trend of economic development at present and in the future. For today's China, after forty years of reform and opening and construction, a large amount of excellent experience has been accumulated. It covers manufacturing, financial trade, and resource development. As the largest developing country with abundant foreign exchange reserves, China has obtained the conditions and capital strength to go out. In this case, Xi Jinping's behavior of putting forward the "One Belt and One Road" initiative on behalf of the world is not only in line with the trend of the times, but also in promoting the peaceful development of the world economy, which will make out of the path of shared prosperity of human destiny, and at the same time, build up the image of a big country and fulfilling the responsibility of the great powers (Hong & Sun, 2016).

Promoting the construction of "One Belt and One Road" is the chorus of China's original and other countries along the road. The construction cooperation of "One Belt and One Road" is a world economy based on the universal development strategy. It seeks to promote exchanges among different regions with an open and inclusive mindset, strengthen strategic cooperation between China and the relevant countries, strengthen the strategic partnership between China and the countries along the road, promote political mutual trust among nations, and create a peaceful and stable surrounding environment for China's development. It can also deepen China's energy cooperation with relevant countries to ensure energy security and accelerate China's energy imports and exports along the line, strengthening China's energy economic ties with Central Asian states, promoting diversification of energy supply and distribution channels, and ensuring collective energy security between China and Central Asian countries (Zhao, 2016).

Therefore, advancing the development of cultural exchanges, trade cooperation and economical construction investment between China and the countries along the line through the "One Belt and One Road" construction will push the "Chinese dream" to the whole world, which helps to promote cooperation between the bridge linking "China dream" and "world dream," and establish a "destiny of Asia Pacific dream" community, leading the world's economic development to a more peaceful and prosperous life. This will lead all people of the world to achieve their dreams of living a more peaceful and prosperous life, to realize the "world dream" of all humankind when efforts are taken to reach the great rejuvenation of the Chinese nation (Tajovsky, 2009).

The construction of "One Belt and One Road" is mainly based on the countries along the road but not limited to this. The "One Belt and One Road" is constructed based on the ancient "land Silk Road" and the "maritime Silk Road." It not only includes states along the two ancient routes but also extends to other countries. Developing countries share most parts of it. It aims at promoting economic cooperation and cultural exchanges among these countries, helping to make effective use of the complementary advantages, dislocation competition and economic capital integration of various countries, and creating a new model of south-south cooperation, regional cooperation and intercontinental cooperation (Zenn, 2015).

The "One Belt and One Road" is essentially a concept and initiative for cooperation and win-win cooperation rather than an entity or mechanism. In line with the principle of pragmatism and efficiency, the "One Belt and One Road" makes full use of the existing cooperation mechanism to innovate cooperation forms and flexibly promote joint development according to the different development priorities and conditions of countries along the line. It does not seek to realize the leading power through the new system design but follows the pragmatic economic cooperation principle of adapting measures to local conditions and project orientation. The third-party market cooperation is an open, inclusive, practical, and useful model of international collaboration, which also embodies the concept of building and sharing jointly of "One Belt and One Road." It helps Chinese enterprises and enterprises in various countries, especially those with developed countries to complement each other, and to inject new kinetic energy into the economic development of third countries, to achieve the win-win effect of "1+1+1>3." China and other countries have made positive results in promoting third-party market cooperation.

On October 25, 2018, the Japanese Prime Minister visited China to hold the first third-party market cooperation forum between China and Japanese, showing Japan's attempts to take part in the "One Belt and One Road" construction by Japanese enterprises taking the first step. Data shows that in 2017, the trade volume between China and Japan exceeded 300 billion US dollars. The voice of Japanese economic circles for China and Japan to strengthen third-party market cooperation, as well as cooperation in environmental protection, scientific and technological innovation, and dealing with aging, is growing. Some Japanese companies, such as Japan Express, the logistics giant in Japan, have taken the lead in participating in extensive cooperation under the framework of "One Belt and One Road." In the coming future, China is willing to work with relevant countries and their enterprises to expand the scope of cooperation in the third-party market, adhere to the concept of building and sharing through consultation, open up markets for investment, production, and operation, actively innovate cooperation modes, and support enterprises to open up new markets through various means such as joint bidding and joint venture so that they can achieve complementary advantages and win-win results.

Promoting the construction of "One Belt and One Road" will inject new vitality into the world economy. The "One Belt and One Road" initiative, which focuses on economic and trade investment, financing, and international capacity cooperation, will bring new impetus to the development of the world economy. Therefore, pushing forward the development of "One Belt and One Road" will change the pattern of the world trade system dominated by Europeans and Americans. China, as the largest cargo trading country, is the largest trade partner of 130 countries and regions in the world. It can drive the "along the way" countries to realize trade optimization and upgrading. It can provide broad market and development space for cooperation for the construction of the countries along "One Belt and One Road." It can pull the investment and financing and economic growth of these countries.

It has an essential pulling effect on the infrastructure demand and industrial upgrading of the countries along the road. China now has more than 3 billion US dollars in foreign exchange reserves and has enough capital to invest in financing infrastructure projects needed for "One Belt and One Road" to assist the development of capitalization in developing countries and developing countries and to solve bottlenecks in infrastructure projects. At the same time, China's capacity to cooperate with other countries along the Belt and the development of financial trade can help developing countries and undeveloped countries to achieve rapid growth.

Conclusion

China will work together to build a "One Belt and One Road" platform and work with all the people of the world. China will surely benefit the people of all countries, especially for the needs of the "One Belt and One Road" development and construction. China will make its end to speed up the opening policy platform and valuable lands of all parts of China, including free trade pilot area, free trade port, cross border economic cooperation zone, and overseas economy. In the process of promoting regional economic integration and building a high standard free trade area with the "one belt and one-way" countries and regions, a substantial free capital market with the content of "One Belt and One Road" as the center has been gradually formed, which strives for the great rejuvenation of the Chinese nation and for the goal of building a community of human destiny. If it is carefully organized and rationally laid out, it will surely be successfully realized.

Notes:

1. On March 17, 2017, the United Nations Security Council, with 15 votes in favor, adopted the 2344th resolution on Afghanistan, unanimously called on the international community to condense the assistance of the Afghan consensus and strengthen regional economic cooperation through the construction of "One Belt and One Road." It urges the parties to provide a safe environment for the "one belt and one-way" construction, to strengthen the development strategy and strategic docking, and to promote cooperation with interoperability and pragmatism. The resolution emphasizes that regional cooperation should be promoted in a spirit of win-win cooperation to effectively promote security, stability, and development in Afghanistan and the region and to build a community of human destiny.
2. It is the highest-level forum that has been put forward by the "One Belt and One Road" after three years, including three parts: the opening ceremony, the round table summit, and the high-level meeting. The first "One Belt and One Road" International Cooperation summit was held in Beijing from May 14 to 15, 2017. It is a crucial home diplomacy activity in 2017 and is of great significance for promoting international and regional cooperation. Twenty-nine foreign heads of state and government, the Secretary-General of the United Nations and the

President of the International Committee of the Red Cross attended the summit forum. About 1500 distinguished guests from all walks of life from more than 130 countries participated in the forum as official representatives. More than 4000 journalists from all over the world have registered to report on the forum. On May 15, 2017, President Xi Jinping of the People's Republic of China hosted the round table summit and announced that China would hold the second "One Belt and One Road" International Cooperation Summit Forum in 2019.

3. The core contents of the Bretton Woods system include the establishment of the International Monetary Fund (IMF), the consultation on International Monetary affairs, the support for financing of the short-term balance of payments deficits of member countries; the direct link between the US dollar and gold, the link between currencies and the US dollar (i.e., "double-link"); the implementation of adjustable fixed exchange rate system; and the abolition of foreign exchange control over current account transactions. The Bretton Woods System (1944-1973) began to function in July 1944 when 44 countries held the United Nations National Monetary and Financial Conference in Bretton Woods, New Hampshire, USA, and signed the Bretton Woods Agreement.

Chapter 3
Cultural Factors in Cross-border E-commerce

Since the 2008 international financial crisis, it has shown a weak global economic situation on the whole. The market economy in Europe and America has developed relatively slowly, and the exchange rate of the Chinese currency RMB has constantly fluctuated. The price of raw materials has been rising, and the costs of the labor force and production factors have been increasing. However, due to the escalation of the China-US trade friction and the influence of multiple factors, the growth rate of China's traditional import and export trade has shown a declining trend. In contrast, the total bilateral trade volume between China and the countries and regions along the Belt and Road has constantly been growing, among which the growth rate of the volume and scale of cross-border e-commerce trade has been rising year by year (Zhu, 2015).

Introduction

Cross-border e-commerce is expanding rapidly in a way that changes the stores in the world. Since 1995, the sales volume of global cross-border e-commerce reached $750,000,000 in 1997, and a year later, that figure rose to $2,300,000,000 (IDC, 1998). According to the U.S. Department of Commerce, it reached $55,000,000,000 in 2003. The revenue of business-to-customer (B2C) transactions was up to 27,300,000,000US Dollars in 2005 (Wolfinbarger and Gilly, 2005). In 2017, the trading volume of the global online retail market amounted to 2,304,000,000,000 US Dollars (China International Electronic Commerce Center, 2018). Some scholars predict that the growth rate of cross-border e-commerce will exceed that of domestic e-commerce in the next few years. By 2022, the sales volume of the global cross-border e-commerce market will reach 627,000,000,000US Dollars (China International Electronic Commerce Center, 2018).

The Belt and Road Initiative, first proposed by China, is not only of great practical significance to China's economic and social development but also exerts increasing influence on the international political and economic structure in the world. In the context of the Belt and Road, cross-border e-commerce is facing a huge market among the countries along the Belt and Road and the vast domestic market in China, resulting in more diversified, multi-level and personalized consumer demand. In the future, cross-border e-commerce is bound to be a new engine to promote China's economic development and prosperity, and a new driving force to support China's industrial upgrading and structural transformation. The implementation of the Belt and Road Initiative has brought unprecedented opportunities for the development of cross-border e-commerce. Central Asia, ASEAN, South Asia, Central, and Eastern Europe, West Asia and North Africa, and other countries and regions along the Belt and Road are important cross-border e-commerce markets for China.

The sixty-five countries along the Belt and Road vary in their cultures and customs. If not handled properly in the communication between cross-border e-commerce platforms, it will get into a passive status, which will not be conducive to the development of cross-border e-commerce between China and the countries along the Belt and Road. Scholars concerning cross-cultural research hold that culture is the mediator or moderator of all behaviors. The most important manifestation of culture is the transformation and reconstruction of the subjective world of human beings. Its achievements will be reflected in people's words and deeds. Cultural difference is a crucial factor that leads to differences among the people, and people will subjectively feel so familiar under the same culture that it will be more likely to communicate with each other. Otherwise, they will explore strangely (Hu, 2010: 223). Besides, people have a natural sense of superiority to the local culture, and a psychological resistance and exclusion to a foreign culture, which is mainly manifested in the fact that contradiction may occur and even intensify in the process of business activities involving communication, negotiation, agreement signing and performance and the interpretation of disputed clauses.

Moreover, due to different environments for social development, China and foreign countries have diverse ways to understand and handle personal privacy. Chinese people have a weak idea in this respect. They hold that mutual familiarity and trust is concretely manifested in the sharing of their own life experience, and the sweets and bitters of life with each other, which tends to obtain a goodwill response from each other. On the contrary, foreigners, especially Westerners, are more independent because of their different educational concepts and traditional ideas. At the same time, they lay more stress on the protection of personal privacy and are relatively conservative or even resistant to sharing individual experiences, family, and living conditions with someone else. For example, in the process of making a transaction, Chinese people often ask about the family or work about the other party to express their intimacy, which is very common in China. But many foreigners think that it infringes on their privacy, and they will feel disgusted with it, thus leading to the abortion of the transaction (Jia, 1997: 67).

Therefore, it will be of great practical significance for the smooth and effective communications between cross-border e-commerce platforms by studying the cultures of the countries and regions along the Belt and Road and applying the cross-cultural theory to understand the psychological and behavioral characteristics of consumers in various cultural backgrounds. The current studies on political and economic systems and engineering and technology, but there is a noticeable lack of investigation on cultural issues. This paper tends to start from cultural factors to analyze the concrete situation and put forward corresponding policy recommendations.

Cultural Issues in Cross-border E-commerce along the Belt and Road

At present, the construction of the Belt and Road initiated by China is shifting from superior design to implementation (Research Group of China Center for International Economic Exchanges, 2017). In this process, the Chinese should not only deepen their understanding of the strategic significance of the Belt and Road Initiative, but also establish a global awareness, strengthen their strategic thinking, make the plan and design in a right manner, and grasp critical projects, enhance risk prevention, pay attention to propaganda by the instructions of Xi Jinping, to exert themselves to draw a realistic painting of the Belt and Road with traditional Chinese characteristics.

Development of Cross-border E-commerce along the Belt and Road with the continuous advancement of The Belt and Road Initiative, cross-border e-commerce has become one of the crucial means for countries along the Belt and Road to trade with each other. Cross-border trade is involved not only in the various political and economic systems of the states but also in the issues concerning engineering, technology, and culture. Frequent transnational transactions worldwide are one of the most prominent features of e-commerce nowadays, which requires the marketing personnel to find correct ways to handle the cross-cultural problems arising from cross-border e-commerce. On the one hand, previous scholars who studied cross-border e-commerce mainly focused on the characteristics of technology and homogeneity, and seldom studied the significance of cultural differences in cross-border e-commerce (Abramson and Hollingshead, 2009). On the other hand, even though most of the studies on cross-cultural issues are involved in cultural differences, only a few studies have considered cultural differences in cross-border e-commerce (Giovannini and Rosansky, 1990). Jin et al. have been aware of the cultural differences between the United States and China. They have been discussing the way to eliminate these differences by the Internet and group mail technology. Still, they are unable to answer the question of how to overcome the problems caused by the differences in business culture, let alone deal with the cultural issues affecting cross-border marketing on the Internet (Jin, Mason, and Yim, 1998).

At the Symposium on the 5th Anniversary of Promoting the Construction of The Belt and Road, Xi Jinping emphasized that the joint advancement of The Belt and Road complied with the inherent requirements of the reform of the global governance system, and highlighted the awareness of a community with a shared future where people help each other and share the rights and liabilities, thereby providing a new idea and a new program for improving the reform of the global governance system. Besides, Xi Jinping stressed that the initiative serves as a solution for China to participate in comprehensive opening-up and cooperation, improve global economic governance, promote joint development and prosperity, and build a community with a shared future for humanity (Commentator of People's Daily, 2018). The Belt and Road, a development initiative with great vision and international significance, is bound to contain a brand-new outlook of economic and social development. During its actual practice, the existing international rules may be unable to meet the needs of the Belt and Road fully, so it is necessary to make breakthroughs and bring forth the new through the old (Mei, 2018: 13-20+27). At the same time, China must also be soberly aware that the process and results of the construction of the Belt and Road will inevitably break through the existing international political structure, thus developing a new international political and economic structure, and that whether the developed western countries led by the United States are willing to see and accept such new construction, the formation of such structure is an objective necessity that does not change with people's will.

There is no doubt that the Belt and Road will advance the transformation of the world from horizontal expansion to vertical excavation. The competitive industries, advantageous systems, and concepts will be more evenly distributed across the globe. In contrast, the balance and inclusiveness of the world will be further enhanced, which will ultimately achieve the goal of benefiting China and the world and the vision of creating a community with a shared future (Su,

2016, 29-38+156-157). But China should also make it clear that the Belt and Road, as an international platform for regional cooperation, will inevitably encounter many difficulties in the course of its construction, so that China must continuously improve and develop it when making great efforts to overcome the challenges to make it a reliable cooperative platform for all countries concerned to achieve joint development and an essential practical platform for promoting the construction of a community with a shared future. In recent years, the Internet and cross-border e-commerce have also made significant achievements in China. According to The China Statistical Report on Internet Development provided by China Internet Network Information Center (CNNIC), there had been up to more than 800 million Internet users in China by the end of June 2018, and the number of mobile Internet users had amounted to 788 million (China Internet Network Information Center, 2018). According to the data of the third quarter of 2017, the trading volume of the online retail B2C market in China was126,500,000,000 US Dollars, with a growth of 39.1% over the same period of last year. The total turnover of Tmall increased by 47% over the same period of the previous year and increased by 7.4% compared with the second quarter, and thus Tmall took the lead in the B2C market with a market share of 59.0%. The integration and balance of online and offline channels will offer a more significant market space to Tmall (http://www.ibaogao.com/, 2018). After years of development and accumulation, the market of the mobile Internet in China is developing towards a balanced and healthy market.

Cultural Issues in Cross-border E-commerce

Cross-cultural, cross-border e-commerce requires the marketing personnel to be aware of cultural differences, to be sensitive to them, as well as to respect the rights concerning consumer culture in various cultures and markets. From an anthropological point of view, all market behaviors have cultural boundaries. Consumer behaviors and business practices are determined by the customs of their times (Hamilton, 1987). As a result, the marketing person needs to have a profound understanding of the cultural environment of the market and conduct cross-cultural marketing, to match the combinations of cross-border e-commerce platforms with consumer preferences, purchasing behavior and the use pattern of products in a potential market, such as the transnational businesses carried out by P&G in Canada in recent years. P&G announced that it would increase its investment in the studies on cultural differences throughout the region and establish a team of 60 members to coordinate the research on the U.S. market, which is a more comprehensive, relevant, and meaningful way to seek various approaches to investigate consumers. Besides, micro-ethnic marketing is one of the numerous cases (Saunders, 2001).

Over the past two decades, international trade in the global market has been soaring. The global marketing environment has enabled marketing managers to realize that the way to do business is playing an increasingly decisive role in diverse cultural backgrounds. In a cross-cultural sense, the effective allocation of products has become a key factor to success in the international community, which has allowed cultural issues to become a key factor affecting the success of cross-border e-commerce. The characteristic of cross-border e-commerce is that the information transmitted is not constrained by time and space but is subject to technology and language. The core controversy in the cross-cultural marketing theory is whether culture has a one-way impact on marketing, which is whether culture is a controllable factor or a non-controllable one. Most of the scholars argue that culture is non-controllable due to its characteristics of sociality, generalization, and abstractness. The research findings in academic circles indicate that consumers in various cultural backgrounds tend to show different consumer behaviors and characteristics. There will be specific cultural differences in terms of values, code of conduct, perception, and social interaction, which will exert an influence on the consumer behavior and preferences of e-commerce consumers (Zhou and Yang, 2011).

The debate on whether marketing should be standardized or adaptable has been going on, and it is just in the ascendant in the field of e-commerce. Although practitioners feel excited to stand in the wave of e-commerce communication and commerce, there are only a few scholars who study the standardization and adaptability of e-commerce networks through observation, most of whom have focused on the enterprises in the United States. Sinkovics, Yamin, and Hassinger investigated 100 companies in Germany, as well as websites in the United States, the United Kingdom, and Latin America, and then analyzed their cultural values. Their findings show that in the relevant market, it is less emphasized in the studies on cultural significance, and thus a certain degree of cultural alienation has arisen (Sinkovics, Yamin and Hossinger, 2007).

It is suggested by some scholars that companies need to strive to build more websites with strong cultural adaptability. At the same time, it is necessary to pay more attention to the language. For example, the White Elephant Battery in China gets into a tricky situation in the US market that nobody cares for it, which is because a white elephant means that a thing is a waste of money because it is entirely useless (Wu and Zheng, 2012). Language is one of the elements of culture. The neglect of cultural differences expressed by language is bound to lead to faults in business. However, it is by no means a recommendation that all the marketing staff adjusts their cross-border e-commerce programs solely by focusing on cultural differences, for adapting to consumers in foreign markets. On the contrary, successful marketing staff should also be adept at identifying similarities in various cultures, in identifying opportunities for implementing a standardized marketing mix.

The Role of Cultural Factors in Cross-border E-commerce

Culture plays a specific role in cross-border e-commerce. To study these influences, we first need to explore the culture itself. Culture itself is defined in diverse ways. One definition, which has been most frequently cited by marketing scholars, was created by anthropologists Philip R. Harris and Robert T. Moran. Under their study, culture defines the self-identity of individuals and people in groups, gives people a sense of belonging, and restricts what people should do and how they should express themselves.

Overview of the Impact of Culture on Cross-border E-commerce

Culture is composed of a set of correlated symbols, codes, and values concerning systematic learning and sharing to guide people's behaviors directly. It is often used by scholars in the studies on market and consumer behavior. Still, marketers and consumers often neglect the depth of the concept and its implications for the analysis of human behavior (Harris and Moran, 1987). E-commerce, a financial transaction carried out through electronic means, usually refers to a means of shopping on e-commerce websites or online stores. It seems as if it was weakly associated with culture, but in fact, it goes hand in hand with culture. E-commerce may be carried out between businesses or between businesses and consumers. From a commercial point of view, e-commerce mainly refers to online marketing or cross-border e-commerce. Whatever way it is done, e-commerce behavior is still the interaction between people in the final analysis. As people are social animals with keen cultural awareness and characteristics, it is self-evident that culture has a significant impact on e-commerce.

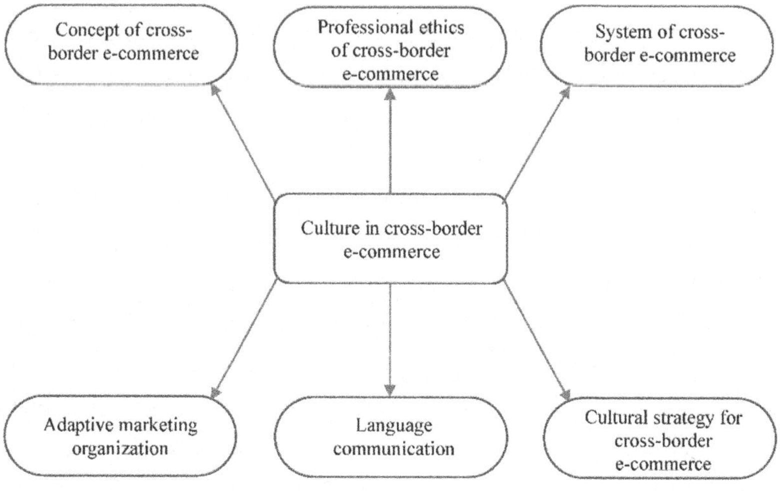

Figure 3.1 Cultural combinations of cross-border e-commerce

The culture in cross-border e-commerce, with the purchasers and consumers of services or products provided by enterprises as the target, is the sum of ideology and code of conduct arising from the handling of the relationship between people and matters, between people and objects, and among people when enterprises are engaged in cross-border e-commerce activities. It includes but is not limited to the following aspects: the concept of cross-border e-commerce, the professional ethics of cross-border e-commerce, the system of cross-border e-commerce, the cultural strategy of cross-border e-commerce, the marketing organization that adapts to the concept and ethics of cross-border e-commerce, and communication in business language and so on (Figure 1). The difference between cross-border e-commerce culture and traditional marketing culture stems from the characteristics or advantages of cross-border e-commerce itself. First, cross-border e-commerce is more conducive to business promotion for enterprises. Second, the development of the Internet has broadened the sphere of marketing. Cross-border e-commerce culture presents guidance in consumption, which allows the competition between Internet companies to rise to a higher level. Most enterprises begin to shift their concerns from the concept of promoting the products to meet consumer demand to the idea of creating demand and initiatively guiding consumption (Ouyang and Zhou, 2006).

According to the survey, there have been up to 751 million Internet users in China, and the figure has grown at a rate of more than 3 million new Internet users per month. The global e-commerce market has multiplied over the past decade, which has been continuing. At present, the number of Internet users around the world has amounted to 4.157 billion, and the Internet penetration rate has reached 54.4%. According to some studies, the number of Internet users in Asia accounts for the most significant proportion of the number of global Internet users, as high as 48.7%. Seven countries have had over 100 million Internet users, among which China is the largest market of Internet users all over the world. From the perspective of the area with a growing number of online shoppers, the fastest-growing areas will be the Middle East and

Africa in the next few years, which are the key areas covered by The Belt and Road Initiative. In 2018, 1.6 billion people will shop on the Internet at least once, accounting for more than 50% of all Internet users. Among them, the online shoppers in the Asia-Pacific region will account for half of the total online shoppers worldwide. In 2017, the trading volume of the global online retail market reached $2.304 trillion, at an increase of 24.8% over the same period last year, and its share in the total volume of global retail sales rose from 8.6% in 2016 to 10.2% (http://www.ec.com.cn/, 2018).

According to eMarketer's research report, the e-commerce industry is becoming increasingly competitive, but Alibaba, a Chinese company, still maintains a leading position. The Double 11 Shopping Festival by Alibaba's shopping sites, Tmall and Taobao, kicked off in 2017. According to the real-time transaction data on November 11, the total volume of the Double 11 Global Shopping Festival in 2017 exceeded ¥ 100,000,000 (about 14,300,000 US Dollars) on Tmall within 11 seconds after the bell sounded at 0 o'clock on November 11, while the wireless transaction accounted for 93%. Within 28 seconds, the turnover exceeded ¥ 1,000,000,000 (about 143,000,000 US Dollars) while the wireless transaction accounted for 97%. In just 3 minutes and 1 second, the turnover exceeded ¥ 10,000,000,000 (about 1,430,000,000 US Dollars).

In contrast, in 2017, Lazada's Double 11 Festival successfully set the trend in the Southeast Asian market, with 6.5 million orders per day and total sales of $120,000,000, an increase of 191% over the same period last year. The sales figure of the Southeast Asian market is dwarfed by China's domestic sales of $25,000,000,000 per day on the Double 11 Shopping Festival. Still, Alibaba and all the e-commerce giants have found business opportunities due to its rapid growth and replicability of its commercial culture and pattern. In 2018, the sales increased every second from 0 o'clock on November 11. With only two minutes and five seconds, the turnover climbed to ¥ 10,000,000,000 (about 1,470,000,000 US Dollars), which was 56 seconds faster to reach the figure compared with the previous year. It only took 107 minutes to exceed ¥ 100,000,000,000 (about 14,700,000,000 US Dollars) seven hours more quickly than the previous year. It took only 15 hours to break the record of ¥ 168, 200,000,000 (about 24,030,000,000 US Dollars) in previous years. The final fixed turnover of ¥ 213,500,000,000 (32,000,000,000 US Dollars) was the first time to achieve a one-day commercial turnover of more than 200 billion yuan (16 billion US Dollars) in the world. In 2018, the sales of Jingdong reached ¥ 159, 800,000,000 (22,830,000,000 US Dollars) on the Double 11 Shopping Festival, which was slightly lower than that of Taobao and Tmall but cannot be underestimated (Yang, 2017). In 2018, Alibaba, the giant of retail e-commerce, still holds a market share of nearly 60%, while Jingdong, ranking second, occupies a market share of 16% (eMarketer, 2018).

Thousands of new traders will register on these e-commerce marketing websites mentioned above every day. The categories of products cover almost the full range of products and services throughout the world. Anyone who clicks into a commercial site for the second time can practically find any type he likes (Bandiwadekar, 2002). Such precise marketing not only dramatically improves the accuracy and hit rate of advertising, saves the advertising cost of e-commerce platforms, but also improves the service level of e-commerce platforms, reduces transaction costs and enhances transaction efficiency, and strengthens the customer delivered value (Li and Jiang, 2013).

There is no doubt that cross-border e-commerce, as an innovative marketing method, has attracted the attention of both the public sector and the private sector in commercial circles. Like traditional marketing, cross-border e-commerce is not only affected by cultural issues but also transforms culture. One of the essential respects where culture affects commerce is import and export trade, which reflects that culture does have an impact on some commercial connection. Such a phenomenon is called cross-cultural marketing in today's business world (Goldman, 1992).

Enhancing of Cognitive Ability towards Cultural Difference

The traditional multi-national marketing methods focus on geographical markets and are willing to concentrate on the development of a unique marketing mix for each market. However, cross-border e-commerce has broken through the geographical constraints, which are mainly reflected in two aspects of increasing efficiency due to economies of scale and increased productivity due to technological accumulation. Both factors can use the same marketing mix in more than one market. Thus, it can be seen that global cross-border e-commerce focuses on the product market, which is needed jointly by consumer groups and emphasizes their similarities regardless of where they live. However, it should not ignore the differences between the markets and must be taken into account within the scope of implementing the marketing plan. For example, marketers' websites should be able to be translated into different languages for the markets in various countries. Different distribution strategies should also be developed for regions with varying structures of distribution. During the period, the novelty of information plays a decisive role in successfully changing consumer attitudes, delivering information content, and attracting consumers (Cao and Xue, 2006).

Therefore, the marketing staff must understand that the Internet has made potential contributions to the marketing process, identify the differences between cross-border e-commerce and traditional marketing, and study more appropriate ways to use the Internet to provide solutions for the demand of global marketing. Unlike the primary task of conventional marketing to define the target market, the target market groups excavated by cross-border e-commerce contain the same content, even though they vary in geographic location. As Bandiwadekar pointed out, to succeed in cross-border e-commerce, the marketing staff must email potential customers and identify them on the Internet, instead of waiting for customers to visit the e-commerce websites. When potential customers are identified, the marketing staff may inform them of the relevant sites or specific links, which will increase the possibility of using the particular products promoted by the marketing staff (Bandiwadekar, 2002).

Cross-border e-commerce allows the labor force, the primary factor of productivity, to enhance its dependence on the ability to acquire, transmit, process and use information in an unprecedented manner and promote the emergence and rapid increase of new workers, namely, information workers. It enables the elements of labor tools that play an active role in the productive forces to become networked and intellectualized. At the same time, the amount of information and knowledge implied in it has increased dramatically, while the information network itself has become a relevant public or dedicated labor tool (Wu, 2000).

It is beyond doubt that the Belt and Road have opened a broad market for Chinese enterprises, offered rare development opportunities, but also posed enormous challenges. A more complex and extensive market means that enterprises will be faced with consumers and customers with various cultural backgrounds, which requires enterprises to have a keen awareness and sensitivity of cultural differences in cross-cultural economic and commercial communications. Intercultural economic and commercial communication refers to economic and business communication between consumers or customers. Their culture is different from that of the marketing staff themselves in at least one essential aspect of culture, such as language, religion, social norms and values, education, and lifestyle. To respect consumers' cultural rights in diverse cultures and markets, the marketing staff should understand and respect consumers' rights to their cultures. If the marketing staff intends to succeed in the cross-cultural market, they must work in a way that they respect the values and cultural rights of consumers. For example, the marketing staff of the western countries needs to respect the requirements of the Chinese government for its national conditions in a specific business situation, which means that they must consider the exceptional environment and characteristics of China. Economic and business communication is never an independent behavior, but a behavior related to all other business or market behaviors. From an anthropological point of view, all market behaviors are restricted by culture, and buying and selling are carried out in the context of culture.

Under the strategic background of The Belt and Road, there will be very extensive prospects and space for the economic and trade cooperation between China and the countries along the Belt and Road based on the existing bilateral and multilateral mechanisms with the relevant countries, and with the help of effective regional cooperation platforms. In the context of such a major revolution, the implementation of The Belt and Road Initiative provides excellent policy support, broad market space, and a relaxing competitive environment for the cross-border e-commerce industry. At the same time, the implementation of The Belt and Road Initiative also requires the cross-border e-commerce industry, which can confront foreign consumers with both cost space and profit advantages, to promote its future implementation and development (Zhu, 2015). In the context of The Belt and Road Initiative, cross-border e-commerce has developed rapidly, which has led to cross-cultural conflicts from time to time. It is an essential feature of cross-border e-commerce to accelerate the understanding of culture and incorporate a broader range of cultural elements. However, in the actual operation process, cultural differences result in inevitable conflicts, resulting in a lower rate of intention achievement and contract signing between e-commerce platforms and customers compared with those in the domestic market, and even some cross-border e-commerce platforms have difficulty in carrying out a cause. The key to solving this problem is to resolve cross-cultural conflicts (Gao, 2018). The essential feature of the target market of cross-border e-commerce is to include those who are related to cross-cultural marketing and those who are in different countries. Therefore, there are some limitations, such as the uncertain credibility of online marketers, lack of adequate distribution channels, and the business-to-business (B2B) marketing model adopted by most of the cross-border e-commerce platforms. Also, companies or companies prohibit or restrict individuals from using their computers and networks, especially those related to shopping and entertainment. Therefore, those who are concerned about cross-border e-commerce are potential customers who have computers and networks at home.

The demographic characteristics of online consumers may be like those of innovators and early adopters in product diffusion theory, who tend to be young, equally educated, and have higher incomes. Abramson and Hollingshead classify Internet users as surfers and shoppers. They believe that surfers use the Internet for entertainment, and they visit the websites for the web pages one after another like explorers. Still, they seldom repeat the same webpage, unless there are some temptations for them. Shoppers usually use the Internet for direct purposes, to get some information on the topics that they are interested in, to make some shopping decisions or to go online shopping (Abramson and Hollingshead, 2009).

Cross-cultural Path of Cross-border E-commerce Combination

The marketing concept emphasizes the importance of satisfying consumers, and the goal of cross-border e-commerce is no exception. However, the rules of cross-border e-commerce have not yet been clearly defined, and the correct institutional factors can ensure that both the marketing staff and consumers are satisfied with online transactions. In this regard, the marketing staff must have a profound understanding of the cultural environment of the market to adapt marketing to consumer preferences, purchasing behavior, and product use patterns. Manufacturers should not focus on cultural differences merely for adjusting the procedures of commercial and business communication so that consumers can accept them. At the same time, it is suggested that enterprises should also pay attention to identifying the similarities between cultures so that they can identify opportunities and modify the standard marketing strategies per the economic and business communication theory with cultural information. It is an essential task for commercial activities to deal with these cultural similarities and differences in a skillful way in the global market.

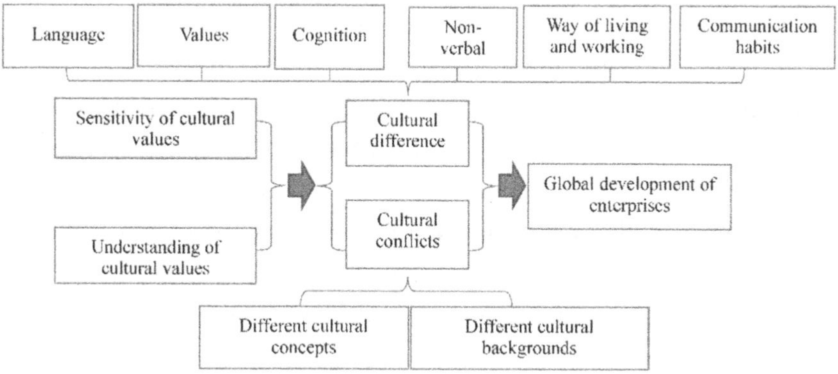

Figure 3.2 Cultural path of the global development of enterprises

Research on Traditional Cross-cultural Marketing

E-commerce is somewhat different from traditional business activities, but there are still some criteria that can be followed. The basic principles of conventional marketing emphasize the 4P combination, namely, product, price, promotion, and place. The 4P combination can also be applied to the cross-cultural strategy for developing cross-border e-commerce. In theory, the priority should be given to the products provided. Consumer products can be classified into featured commodities, shopping products, and convenience goods. The target group of featured commodities is consumers who have specific preferences and are willing to make significant efforts to obtain the commodities. At present, the most significant opportunity to provide featured specialties is to sell them on the Internet. At the same time, customers are aware of seeking them based on their demand, and they are even loyal to the brands to a certain degree (Nickels and Wood, 2000). The Internet is also an excellent place to look for things that are hard to find, such as out-of-print books or records by unknown singers. For example, the World Wide Web is a large online market where consumers can find whatever goods they need and can inquire about as they wish. Like Alibaba, it is a multi-product trading site, and initiatively offers the quantity and price of products on sales.

There are also a considerable number of users registering on the site (Bandiwadekar, 2002). The current business scale of Netrepreneurs is advancing from the grade of 10 trillion to that of 100 billion, and Netrepreneurs have gradually penetrated all aspects of economy, society, and life. In the new era, the development of Netrepreneurs is characterized by generalization, pluralism, and complexity, while there are no longer online or offline Netrepreneurs (Ali Research Institute, 2017). The goods purchased online are those that customers are willing to spend a lot of time and energy on in the process of purchasing. Still, these intrinsic goods lack the opportunity for inspection, while the products purchased on the Internet are those that show a gap from customers' expectations.

On the other hand, it can easily accept specification customization and large-scale standardization. For example, buying computers online is a specific advantage of the Internet. Also, consumers will consider searching for the goods they want to buy in the broader range if they're going to buy it at the best price. Convenience goods are goods that are often purchased. Buyers are only willing to make the least effort to obtain such products. At present, there are few opportunities for these goods to be marketed online. Customers buy convenience goods on impulse, which is a severe defect caused by a delay in purchasing decision-making relative to the availability of consumption or service. It is less likely for consumers to realize that they need to add another category of products when they are browsing on the Internet and looking at one of the three types of products. It is also necessary for the marketing staff to keep in mind that a specific product may be categorized as a store-bought good based on one culture. Still, it may also be classified as a featured commodity based on another culture (Tian and Wang, 2014).

For example, bicycles, one of the most popular means of transportation in China, can also be regarded as store-bought goods. Still, they must be considered as featured commodities in the United States. Also, products that do not belong to other categories in the traditional classification may belong to sensitive or personal goods.

Customers who buy goods online are allowed to continue to keep their privacy if they do not provide personal contact information but receive high-quality services. These products, such as sex-related products or services, may require consumers from the United States, Canada, and some Western European countries to buy them on the Internet. However, these types of products are less popular and are banned in some Eastern European countries and the Muslim-dominated markets in the Middle East (Tian and Wang, 2014).

In cross-cultural communication, the essential concern is how to avoid cultural conflicts. Intercultural conflict refers to the mutual exclusion and opposition between different forms of cultures or cultural elements. It may be the conflict arising from the diverse cultural concepts between the transnational enterprises and the host country when the enterprises operate in such state, or the conflict within the enterprise arising from various cultural backgrounds of the employees. Cross-cultural business communication is mainly carried out among people with different cultural backgrounds. Price is one of the essential elements in a marketing mix, as it provides the most obvious basis for comparison. Consumers who buy goods on the Internet may quickly evaluate a great many possible options for commodities based on the price. However, many Internet providers operate in two modes of regular physical stores and virtual stores on the Internet. These modes of operation are likely or unlikely to achieve lower costs, especially in most developing countries. Another price advantage that Internet shoppers can enjoy is that they do not need to pay the sales tax on the goods purchased and delivered by cross-border express. When the cost of delivery is added to the pick-up price, it will discount the interests of consumers. The number of goods purchased and delivered on the Internet may rise because of the transportation cost (Abramson and Hollingshead, 1999).

Cross-cultural Thinking in Cross-border E-commerce

The Internet is originally a means of communication since it can provide more promotional advertisements for customers as an advertising medium. From the perspective of customers, the problem is to find the appropriate seller's website, which is similar to looking for a Chinese restaurant in a strange city. One way is to walk around the city and hope to find a restaurant providing delicious Chinese food. Such a non-directional strategy is similar to the idea that Internet surfers wander between web pages to find something interesting. For shoppers who choose their preferred destination by checking some form of index or catalog, a more effective strategy is to find the place they need using the map navigator. Online shoppers can identify potential suppliers through search engines or classified directories, which indicates that the websites should be listed in as many search engines as possible with appropriate translations to succeed in cross-border e-commerce. Besides, propagandists can link relevant materials and prominent advertisements on popular websites to make it easier for consumers to access the supplier's location and thus establish some transactions with potential customers. Besides, advertisements on traditional media can also be used to guide people to visit sites on the Internet.

In the context of building a community with a shared future, the layout and implementation of China's The Belt and Road Initiative and the establishment of the Asian Infrastructure Investment Bank undoubtedly narrow the gap between China and other countries in the world and bring about more opportunities for Chinese enterprises to engage in cross-border trade. Cultural factors play an essential role in cross-national communication. When the world has become increasingly globalized, many countries are paying more and more attention to preserving their features. We are justified to predict, as always, that national culture will continue to be a critical factor in the process of globalization and will affect national trade policy, intellectual property protection, creation of resources for state interests, and other aspects. At a more micro level, cultural differences will cause some invisible obstacles to the enterprises developing globally (Ming, 2018).

From the consumer's point of view, one of the shortcomings of Internet shopping is the lack of privacy and security. It is likely for consumers to feel dissatisfied when buying goods online, as some of the products may be of poor quality, falsely publicized, or merely a fraud. Two feasible ways to alleviate consumer concerns are that merchants have transparent and fair return policies and that the credit card companies provide payment guarantees for customers. In the case of the goods delivered by mistake of credit card, the company can issue a credit card to alleviate the consumer's liabilities for consumer credit. The ultimate concern of consumers is transaction security. Sometimes credit card information is inaccurately accessed, which will lead to credit card companies charging consumers a large number of wrong fees. Credit card issuers in developed countries can reduce these risks by improving the security of electronic transmission and issuing some more extensive protection policies. However, for developing countries, it takes a long time to formulate and implement these policies. Thus, it is not yet apparent in the capacity and opportunities of cross-border e-commerce in the foreseeable future.

Cross-border E-commerce

For the business personnel who are engaged in transnational marketing, they need to keep in mind that in business practice, they must have a precise understanding of the local cultural values and maintain an individual sensitivity to the local cultural values if they want to succeed in the target market. It is of great significance for the marketing staff to get help from the local business circles and cooperate with them. The best way to remain sensitive to local cultural values is to identify who will be the intended target audience. However, the marketing staff even inevitably makes some mistakes, as they often neglect the local cultural values. The marketing staff of Nike's and Giant's sports shoes appeals to China's national pride through promotion strategies rather than using the typical American advertisements to increase its market share in China. Nike's practice has not only shown its considerable sensitivity to Chinese consumers but also shocked Chinese government officials. It also hired the Art Director and clerical staff in China to prepare its business plan following the

Chinese culture, rather than imposing American culture on the Chinese people (Warner, 1997).

Internet users can browse almost any website on the Internet. One of the problems in web design is the conflict between creativity and profit. Those who are creative desire to create expressive advertisements and sites with artistic values, while sales managers may just want the advertisement to help the salespersons sell their products. The purpose of using advertisements and websites is to make it easier for consumers to choose tasks, which means that information will be easily found and downloaded and that the website will be more readily understood and used. In this way, it is necessary to make websites in several languages, as well as make some modifications to the websites to meet the needs of cross-cultural communication.

The Internet is not only a medium of communication but also has the advantage of simple transactions. Consumers can select substitute suppliers and products in their minds on the computer, place orders, and make payments, all of which can be done by computers. The easy-to-use feature may be the most potent factor in promoting consumers to buy goods on the Internet. Soon, such easy-to-use performance will increase with the advancement of technology. On the one hand, Internet shoppers can easily buy what they want at home. On the other hand, shoppers can access every corner of the world by the computer, and customers can quickly and continuously visit a website from diverse cultural backgrounds, which requires the marketing staff to be prepared for answering the questions posed by customers from entirely different cultural backgrounds.

Most of the conventional wisdom regarding retail can help to achieve customer satisfaction on the Internet. Customers are usually impressed by the appearance of the online store for the first time. In case of a wrong impression, the customer will not buy anything in the store, nor will he revisit it as far as the most durable material style of web design, the layout, atmosphere, appearance or image of the website, whether material or virtual, are all aimed at facilitating customers and turning the website into the key to attracting consumers from diverse cultural backgrounds to shop on the site. Despite possible additional costs, such additional charges will be bound to create some businesses with higher added value in the long run, thus ultimately enabling those who take steps earlier in this respect to become winners in cross-cultural Internet marketing.

At present, there is still a lack of the ultimate solution to security in online shopping, and most of the people in the world are still unable to access the Internet. There are several limitations to the cross-border e-commerce industry. Soon, there will a substantial increase in the online business, but many retailers may still operate in two modes of a physical store and an online store. These two-sided operations complement each other. They exist in the appropriate market and work on a cross-functional and cross-cultural basis.

Conclusions

Under the impetus of The Belt and Road Initiative and the influence of macro and microeconomic factors at home and abroad, cross-border e-commerce has achieved a favorable trend and scale of development. The development and rise of cross-border e-commerce are conducive to promoting the structural upgrading and transformation of emerging industries, the deepening of cooperation and exchanges between surrounding areas and the free trade areas, as well as the development of domestic and foreign investments and foreign trade economy. China should face up to many of its problems and restrictions in terms of the transformation of industrial chain, the supporting services of cross-border e-commerce and the building of its brands, find and solve issues promptly, make rational plans, and focus on innovation and coordinated development, thereby providing pleasant policy environment and development space for enterprises engaged in cross-border e-commerce and contributing to the growth and prosperity of cross-border e-commerce (Zhu, 2015).

The communication expressway, the Internet, reshapes the business environment and presents opportunities and challenges to the marketing staff. Exporters, importers, international brokers, and other parties concerned also take advantage of the low cost of the Internet to carry out foreign trade. Internet information services are also of some value to existing products or services, which can help to develop marketing channels and formulate strategies. Like traditional marketing, cross-border e-commerce is not only affected by cultural issues but also transforms culture. These two aspects reflect a common phenomenon, which is known as cross-cultural marketing in today's business world. From an anthropological point of view, all market behaviors have cultural boundaries. Consumer behaviors and business practices are determined by the cultures of their times. From an anthropological point of view, the author analyses the role of the Internet in marketing and the cross-cultural phenomena and problems in cross-border e-commerce. Based on the influence and function of culture in traditional marketing, this Chapter discusses the concept of national advertising in cross-border e-commerce, which is deemed to be an excellent method of cross-cultural marketing worth promoting.

Chapter 4
Innovated Views of Economic and Social Development

To realize the great rejuvenation of the Chinese nation is the greatest dream for the Chinese people since the beginning of the last century. The "Chinese dream" is a significant historic economic and social project that requires all the Chinese people to work hard together along with the people in the "One Belt One Road" countries. Since the reform and opening started 40 years ago, considerable achievements have been made in China's economic and social development, although there are problems that need to be resolved. It is undoubtedly necessary to explore the causes of the issues and put forward strategies to remedy the defects. To realize the Chinese dream, Chinese people need to innovate the concept of economic and social development, so that to create a new type of country with more muscular comprehensive national strength and finally realize the dream of the great rejuvenation of the Chinese nation.

Introduction

In 2012, President Xi Jinping put forward the strategic concept of the "Chinese Dream" to realize the great rejuvenation of the country, the prosperity of the nation, and the happiness of people. The realization of this concept will be a great leap forward in the chronicle history of China (Li, 2012). According to the thinking of Xi Jinping, the "Chinese Dream" embodies the long-cherished aspirations of generations of Chinese people, represents the overall interests of the Chinese nation and the Chinese people, which is the common aspiration of every Chinese son and daughter and is a great project for the benefit of the Chinese nation for thousands of generations to come (Guo, 2014). The Chinese dream is not isolated and not connected with the outside world, but it shares the dreams of people all over the world. Undoubtedly, the reform and opening have greatly enhanced China's comprehensive national strength and provided a broader space for China's rise and the creation of the Chinese miracle. The organic unity of the "Chinese Dream" and the "Community of Shared Future for Mankind" is the focus of political and economic construction in the new era. China must also realize that the competition of the comprehensive national strength of all countries in the world is becoming more and more intense, so China is facing many challenges. There are also many problems in the construction of socialism with Chinese characteristics, among which roads, theoretical issues, system issues, and cultural issues are the core issues. How to seize the opportunities and meet the challenges has become the most pressing issue facing the Chinese government and people.

The realization of the "Chinese Dream" is a very complicated economic and social development project. In this process, China needs to be able to deal with many complex and changeable things, continually absorb ancient and modern ideas at home and abroad and innovates a higher and more intelligent art of guidance. Under the leadership of correct theories, the effect of "right direction," "high efficiency," and "good outcome" can be achieved (Tian & Dai, 2012). It is also very important to understand that the "One Belt One Road" initiative reflects the international factors of the Chinese Dream. According to Xi Jinping, the construction of "One Belt One Road" is an important and organic part of realizing the Chinese dream. There must be difficulties and challenges. Only by striving to overcome difficulties and face the challenges can China accomplish the great project of the Chinese dream and realize the great rejuvenation of the Chinese nation.

Achieving the Chinese Dream Requires Correct Theoretical Guidance

Marx pointed out in the preface of *Das Kapital* that the development of social and economical form is a natural and historical process (Marx, 1975). Human society is an organic unity of economic, political, cultural forms, and natural environment. Marx has described various social structures in detail in his classical works. He predicted that society would provide opportunities for people to display their creative abilities in an all-round way instead of limiting human development to a narrow range. Human beings have also summed up the fundamental laws of material civilization, political civilization, spiritual enlightenment, and ecological civilization through various and multi-level experiences and lessons in social practice. Excellent and brilliant achievements have been reached through implementing various practical activities conforming to the objective laws. In China's modernization drive, the understanding of the "four civilizations (namely material, political, spiritual and ecological civilizations" is particularly profound. In the process of human social development, the universal law of its development embodies that the "four civilizations" are mutually conditional, mutually purposeful and mutually reinforcing (Huang & Shen, 2012). Among them, once political civilization and spiritual civilization are formed, they have relative independence and historical inheritance with their particularities of development. Therefore, the realization of the Chinese dream must be guided by the theories of developing socialism with Chinese characteristics and must be based on the particular national conditions of China, be realistic, and conduct a detailed analysis of specific issues.

President Xi Jinping once pointed out that innovation has always been a vital force to promote the development of a country and a nation. He believes that China is a big developing country and is vigorously promoting the transformation of the model of economic growth and the adjustment of economic structure. Thus, the nation must implement the strategy of innovation-driven development well, promote inclusive innovation centered on scientific and technological innovation, adhere to the direction of demand orientation and industrialization, subscribe to the dominant position of enterprises in innovation, and make full use of the decisive role of the market in the allocation of resources and the institutional advantages of socialism, to enhance the contribution of scientific and technological progress to economic growth, form new sources of growth power, and promote sustained and healthy economic development (Li, 2010). The period from 2006 to 2020 is a critical stage of China's socialist economic construction. The Chinese people are facing not only the ever-changing international situation but also rare opportunities for peaceful world development. The realization of the "Chinese Dream," on the one hand, requires a hard struggle to significantly enhance the ability of independent national innovation as well as several scientific and technological achievements that have a significant impact on the world to promote steady economic and social development, to safeguard national security, and to provide strong support for the general construction of a beautiful and happy home. On the other hand, China is required to have an elevated level of material and spiritual civilization to achieve a substantial increase in social productivity to rank at the forefront of the core competitiveness of the world (Liu & Li, 2018). Therefore, developing socialism with Chinese characteristics and building an innovative country are mainly embodied in the following aspects:

Autonomous innovation is the foundation

The 21st century is an era of the rapid development of science and technology, as well as the continuous emergence of inventions and creations. The competition between countries is essentially the competition between broad national powers represented by the level of economics, military, and culture. In recent years, the comprehensive national strength of China has developed to a certain extent, which still has a particular gap compared with the United States and other developed countries (See Table 1 for details). Without the ability of autonomous innovation, it is difficult for the development of the country to break through the restrictions of various intellectual property barriers and to fundamentally solve the significant strategic problems faced by its construction and national security. The word "autonomous" in front of innovation emphasizes that Chinese intellects are the main body of change, which requires China to complete the process of scientific and technological innovation through its efforts so that it can acquire independent intellectual property rights, upgrade the technical level of national industry, and master the core technology in some fields.

Table 4.1 GDP ranking and growth of relevant countries in 2018

GDP Ranking	Country	Billion (US dollars)	Billion (China Yuan)	The growth rate in 2018
1	U.S. A	19362.13	130810.6	1.27%
2	China	12945.41	82712.19	12.25%
3	Japan	4884.49	32999.61	2.01%
4	Germany	3651.87	24672.03	1.38%
5	France	2574.81	17395.42	1.12%
6	Britain	2565.05	17329.48	2.08%
7	India	2439.01	16477.95	12.78%
8	Brazil	2080.92	14058.7	3.30%
9	Italy	1921.14	12979.22	2.02%
10	Canada	1640.39	11082.47	4.07%

Source: National Bureau of Statistics

Xi Jinping emphasized autonomous innovation when he visited the Guangdong-Australia Cooperative TCM Science and Technology Industrial Park in Hengqin New Area, pointing out the significance of accelerating the enhancement of the ability and strength of autonomous innovation and emphasizing the development of the real economy. Independent change is the foundation of national economic and social development, the strong driving force of national development, and the indispensable lifeline for the survival and development of the Chinese nation. Only by enhancing the ability of inclusive innovation from the global perspective of a broader world, can China win the first place in basic science and frontier technology research, enhance key technologies and strengthen the core competitiveness, promote comprehensive national strength to form strong governance and to seize opportunities, calmly respond to various challenges, and strive to advance the cause of socialism with Chinese characteristics.

Shared prosperity is the goal

The goal of realizing the Chinese dream is the prosperity of the country, the revitalization of the nation, and the happiness of the people. The realization of the "Chinese Dream" of the great rejuvenation of the Chinese nation and the construction of a win-win "Community of the Shared Future for Mankind" are essential components of Xi Jinping's socialist thought with Chinese characteristics in the new era, which are organically integrated into the political construction of socialism with Chinese features at present (Dong & Su, 2018). Forty years of the reform and opening have yielded fruitful results, which have confirmed this correct political understanding. In the process of developing socialism with Chinese characteristics and building an innovative country, the Chinese people are not only the main body of the practice of autonomous innovation but also the beneficiaries and sharers of the achievements of independent innovation. The cumbersome task of historical transformation lies in their shoulders, which should be equipped with Mao Zedong's pioneering spirit of "Yu Gong Yi Shan." The people should be fully involved in the process of formulating reform plans and designs, innovative ideas and fresh impetus from ordinary people should be fully absorbed, all "left," and "right" speech interference that hinders the construction of socialist market economic system with Chinese characteristics should be removed, people's minds and drums should be emancipated, innovation should be encouraged so that the peak can be reached bravely. As far as the current economic and social situation is concerned, there are joys and sorrows. The people have personally realized the happiness brought about by the reform and opening-up, so they sincerely support the improvement with pleasure. At the same time, there are also some problems among which the gap between the development level of the South and the north, as well as the widening difference between the West and the East, attracts people's attention most. Besides, the gap between the actual disposable income of urban and rural residents also continues to widen (see Table 2 for details).

Table 4.2 Changes in per capita disposable income of urban and rural residents from 2013 to 2018

Year	2013	2014	2015	2016	2017	2018
Per capita disposable income of urban residents (RMB)	26,467	28,844	31,195	33,616	36,396	39,251
Per capita disposable income of rural residents (RMB)	9,430	10,489	11,422	12,363	13,432	14,617
Per capita Disposable Income Difference between Urban and Rural Residents (RMB)	17,037	18,355	19,773	21,253	22,964	24,634

Source: National Bureau of Statistics

In addition to the widening income gap, there are also some problems in other areas, such as the inconvenience caused by the absence of public services, uneven distribution of educational resources, endless disputes between doctors and patients, and so on. These situations are unprecedented problems in past economic construction. Therefore, the Chinese should use innovative thinking and exploring ways to find solutions to these problems. In the final analysis, improving people's sense of happiness and making them truly feel satisfied is the real link of cohesion of our China's strength and the safety valve of Chinese society. Through active reform practices that weeds out the old by bringing forth the new, continues to expand the opening to the outside world, and deepens the reform of the economic system, some deep-seated problems exposed will be solved to ensure the legitimate rights and interests of the people, and allow the reform results to be shared collectively (Tian & Dai, 2012).

New rural construction is the critical point

Since the Third Plenary Session of the Eleventh Central Committee of the Communist Party of China was held in 1978, the reform began in the countryside and soon swept across the whole country. In March 2016, the 13th Five-Year Plan pointed out: "Agriculture is the basis for building a well-off society in an all-round way and realizing modernization. China must speed up the transformation of agricultural development mode, focus on building a modern system of the agricultural industry, production and management, improve the efficiency and competitiveness of agricultural quality, and take the road of agricultural modernization with high output efficiency, excellent product safety, reasonable resource conservation and environment-friendly system (Niu, 2016)." The plan emphasizes that economic work should focus on rural areas, vigorously building and developing new countryside construction, and implementing a precise poverty alleviation policy.

At present, China's agriculture not only bears the supply of commodity grain and oil for the survival of the world's largest population but also carries the enormous competitive pressure brought about by the integration of the world economy. Therefore, China should use the scientific development concept to explore and analyze problems, use innovative technologies, methods, and policies suitable for China's rural areas to guide and promote agricultural development, create green GDP, and implement new rural construction. In this course, deepening the reform of the economic system is very important. China should reform all unreasonable regulations and systems that block autonomous innovation, form a social atmosphere that encourages innovating independently and establishing and improving the institutional mechanism that encourages independent innovation. Only in this way can China seize the opportunity, enhance the ability of autonomous innovation, and realize industrial restructuring (Li & Gao, 2013). Therefore, China should focus on solving the problems left over by the history of rural education and newly emerging challenges and cultivate talents for the construction of a new countryside. As the rural area is vast with various situations and robust, the government should reform the working methods, promote the administration according to laws, speed up the construction of the rule of law and the service-oriented and effective government, and promote the continuous development of pastoral work.

Be brave to participate in world market competition

The competition in the world market is a war without smoke. China needs to complete autonomous innovation with high-spirited posture and struggling spirit to occupy the commanding heights in the international economic competition. Compared with the emerging high-tech level represented by patented technology in the developed countries of the world, the overall level of science and technology in China is still at a superficial level (see Fig. 4.1 for details). Faced with such a reality, China must face the competition of commercial science and technology, keep climbing, and persist in what the Chinese are doing. In Japan, the high-tech industry is regarded as being technology-intensive, fast-renewable, and effectively resource-saving. It has formed an absolute scale of the market, which can penetrate and drive the development of other related industries (Yu, 2010).

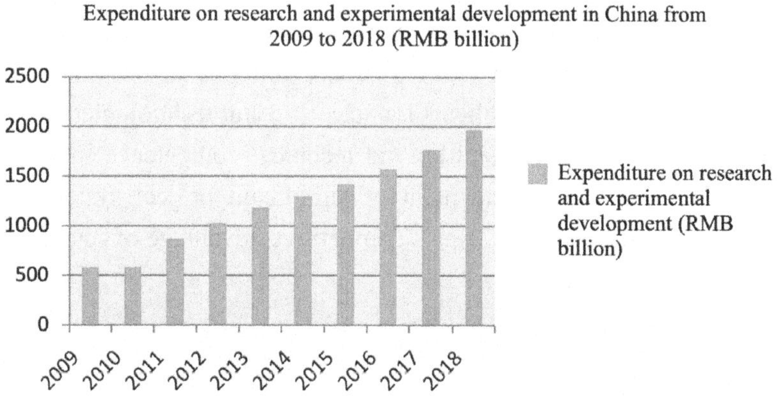

(RMB billion, based on data from the National Bureau of Statistics)

Figure 4.1 Expenditure on research and experimental development in China from 2009 to 2018

Therefore, insisting on autonomous innovation and reflecting the achievements of it through product manufacturing of enterprises can help to occupy an essential part of the industrial chain of world economic integration. Otherwise, it will be ruthlessly eliminated by the market because of the loss of vitality. Individual efforts should be devoted to tracking the fields of technological inventions dedicated to developed countries and keeping up with them. In the field of science, which is of considerable significance to national development and security, China should seek new technological breakthroughs, concentrate their efforts on tackling fundamental problems, and continuously expand the share of the international market under the principle of suitability for national conditions and strength characteristics.

Since China joined the WTO in 2001, it has entered the competition of the international commercial market on a large scale. The total import and export volume has increased significantly. It produces some products with independent intellectual property rights to meet the demand of the world market. In the field of high-tech, there are launches of commercial satellite, shipbuilding industries, and so on. In the area of consumer goods, clothing, toys, hardware, tourist shoes, and products of other businesses made in China have been sold all over the world, and China has become the "world factory" in this field (see Table 4.3 for details) (Sun, 2011). China should continue to formulate new, targeted, and operational policies for scientific and technological reform. The state should guide scientific and technical competence in general projects through the management of significant project systems and market systems, to ensure China's competitive advantage of science and technology at various levels.

Table 4.3 China's total import and export volume from 2009 to 2017

Year	Total import and export volume (RMB billion)	Total export volume (RMB billion)	Total imports (RMB billion)	Import and Export Balance (RMB billion)
2009	15,064.806	8,202.969	6,861.837	1,341.132
2010	20,172.234	10,702.284	9,469.95	1,232.334
2011	23,640.195	12,324.056	11,316.139	1,007.916
2012	24,416.021	12,935.925	11,480.096	1,455.829
2013	25,816.889	13,713.143	12,103.746	1,609.398
2014	26,424.177	14,388.375	12,035.803	2,352.572
2015	24,550.293	14,116.683	10,433.61	3,683.073
2016	24,338.646	13,841.929	10,496.717	3,345.212
2017	27,810.1	15,331.119	12,478.981	2,852.138

Source: National Bureau of Statistics

At present, China's economy has reached a relatively large scale, and the reform has entered a critical stage, beginning to touch the "bone" that is difficult to handle. Continuing to maintain the growth rate of the national macroeconomic economy and operating in the low price rising range is the focus of the national strategy at present and in the future. China should creatively implement macro-control policies to improve some structural problems in economic operation further, alleviate the contradiction between energy and its transportation, and further promote socialism with Chinese characteristics.

Eliminate the Influence of the "Pan-Marketization" Thought Trend

As the purpose of developing socialism with Chinese characteristics is to realize the Chinese dream, build an innovative country and enhance comprehensive national strength, it inevitably involves all aspects of domestic affairs, needs to mobilize positive factors in all aspects, and adopt appropriate construction and management methods for different specific areas. However, according to the basic principles of Marxism, the economic development of a country has objective regularity. People need to adopt appropriate methods to act according to this regularity and give full play to their subjective initiative within the allowable scope of the balance. Other social fields also have their social values and development laws, so the way people act should be regulated by corresponding theories.

Developing a socialist market economy is undoubtedly an effective way to realize the Chinese dream. However, the market economy is not equal to "pan-marketization." The so-called "pan-marketization" tendency mainly refers to the gradual trend towards the market operation of some basic and public welfare departments such as science, education, culture, and health. However, when general welfare sectors such as health and education are "pan-marketized," the problems in the reform of the economic system are severe. The aim of adhering to the principle of the reform about the socialist market economy is to hope that China's educational concept can be innovatively developed, quality education can be implemented for all, and educational equity can be ensured. Therefore, to remove the obstacles to the realization of the Chinese Dream, China must be conscious of the evil influence of the thoughts about the "pan-marketization" trend.

Trading principles should not be applied in the field of public service

It is undeniable that one of the essential goals of the reform is to establish a socialist system of the market economy with Chinese characteristics that are compatible with the current situation of China. Article 15 of the Constitution of the People's Republic of China (namely, the revised version adopted by the Second Session of the Tenth National People's Congress on March 14, 2004) stipulates that "the state should implement socialist market economy." Before the reform, the Chinese government implemented an economic policy by "giving priority to a planned economy, supplemented by market economy" and "carrying out planned commodity economy." The reform guideline approved by the National People's Congress conforms to both the

Marxist value system and China's national conditions (Sun, 2004). Based on the severe reflection on the theory and practice of social and economic development in China before the reform, the reform path was finally determined in the form of the Constitution. In the past, under the single planned economy system, people's interpretation of market information is easily influenced by one-sidedness such as subjective understanding, and their narrow personal will easily dominates market activities.

In contrast, the violation of market law will inevitably lead to the distortion of the economic market and causes difficulties for market law to play an objective role. It is necessary to understand and respect the market law scientifically, and to change the abnormal and distorted old economic system. The government should honestly act according to market law so that the market can play a fundamental role in the allocation of resources. By doing so, numerous factors of production can flow through the market, and the distribution of resources can be optimized, transaction costs can be reduced. In this way, China can improve the operational efficiency of the whole economic system. Therefore, it is necessary to continue to adhere to the reform (Sun, 2010).

With the rise of Pan-market reform, people regard profit-seeking and maximization of capital gains as the only principle to regulate social relations among people, which disturbs people's rational analysis and scientific thinking of national conditions. The actual market-oriented reforms carried out in some places have shown visible characteristics of reducing the proportion of the state-owned economy and strengthening the share of privatization. Eventually, many state-owned enterprises have been sold cheaply, resulting in a significant loss of state-owned assets. If such practices are not corrected or stopped but can develop, the ruling foundation of the state power will be severely eroded by the hidden crisis. The long-term method of socialist construction has also clearly shown that in the areas such as the leadership system, government agencies, ideological theory, judicial, military, ethnic and religious affairs of the Communist Party of China and the republic country, in-depth reform cannot be "market-oriented," and that those departments cannot have any tendency towards privatization. Improvements in the fields of science and technology, education, culture, sports, medical treatment, health, and environmental protection cannot be privatized entirely on the principle of "market orientation." Similarly, for the reform of a large number of non-profit organizations and non-governmental organizations that already exist in society, China should also eliminate the tendency of overall privatization oriented by market, since that would be tantamount to indulgence, which would only weaken the ruling power of the Communist Party, make the so-called rights and interests of vested interest groups over-inflate and endanger the fundamental importance of the people (Liu, 2007).

Even in the economic field, for the sake of national security and public social interests, there will inevitably be some public resources and public goods that are impossible or not allowed to be traded through the market, let alone be privatized. The popular economics textbooks of American universities point out that "the materials or funds to produce of public goods such as defense and armaments should be controlled by the government" (Mcconnell, 2005). Can China marketize and privatize its defense industry? The answer is negative, and the same is valid for all countries in the world. Moreover, a real market economy necessarily needs a market environment with equal status of market players, open and transparent market rules, standardized and orderly trading process, fair and reasonable market management, and the appropriate market environment under the rule of law. The consequences of the privatization of key industries related to the national economy and people's livelihood, such as the domestic defense industry, are unimaginable. The implementation of the so-called completely free "marketization" of a private economic system is impossible in contemporary human society. Therefore, to continue to deepen the reform of the economic system, China must strengthen the national management, conduct economic and social activities following the objective laws of the economy, obtain the best social and economic results using as few resources as possible and the optimal combination, and make an effort to coordinate the development of economic and social environment. China must never allow the reform of the "self-improvement of the socialist system" to be distorted into "market-oriented reform" as such misleading is not so much childish as ulterior motives (Liu, 2013).

Extreme Negative Benefits of the "Pan-marketization" Theory

In real life, the degree of marketization is not enough. For example, some of the market regulation has not yet been given to the market, which leaves many loopholes for the "pan-marketization" phenomenon to succeed. A typical example is an argument of "high salary nourishes integrity." Compared with countries with a long history of market economy system, the salaries of civil servants in Chinese governmental institutions are relatively low. In common sense, public servants should have wages commensurate with their status and contributions. Their hard-work should be reasonably rewarded, and the remuneration should increase along with the development of the economy.

Nevertheless, this does not mean that high salary nourishes integrity. The "high salary nourishes integrity" theory refers to a market trading principle, which is, to buy integrity for the public at a high price. It is not advisable to apply the law of market transactions to the political field. Honesty, as a noble act, cannot enter the market transactions, nor can it be bought with money. In political life, market principles should not be adopted. The Chinese should emphasize politics, responsibility, and morality rather than cash. It is undeniable that the trend of "pan-marketization" has brought troubles to our country and nation. In the process of reform, the starting point of the so-called "pan-marketization" argument completely deviates from the interests of the state and the government at the very beginning, by the fallacies of which the economic and social chaos that once appeared in some regions (Tian, Dai & Qi, 2012).

What needs to be reflected and corrected is that some local administrators even interpret marketization as the privatization of the whole society and the government's getting rid of the burden. Under the guise of "market-oriented operation," some functional departments of local government have abandoned many responsibilities they should assume, and not to mention that the market is full of "counterfeit and inferior" products and "pitfalls and abductions." Even some public schools, hospitals, and institutions engaged in general welfare undertakings have rightly begun to carry out "market-oriented reform" for the sake of "money" and "interests." What is more chilling is that some government agencies are also trying to use their power in hand as "capital" in exchange for some of the interests that are biased or in line with the nature of small groups. In many places and units, the allocation of public resources has been transformed into their interests through "market-oriented operation." The market principles of "capitalization of power" and "equivalent exchange of values" are also widely used in officialdom. Corrupt cases of buying or escaping officials, as well as embezzlement of public funds, occur quite frequently.

What is more worrying is that in the process of pan-marketization, the pace of economic transformation in some places is too abrupt. Without other alternative measures, many workers in public enterprises and rural farmers have lost many of their social benefits, including labor insurance and retirement benefits for urban workers and labor subsidies for rural peasants in the period of communes. Besides, the measures of "buyout of the length of service" in some local enterprises are also very inappropriate as numerous laid-off workers and their families have been affected. The number of laid-off workers affected by these measures is enormous, making the problem of employment, which has been very acute and prominent, even worse, thus forming potential and a destructive army of laid-off unemployed workers. Moreover, due to the bankruptcy of small and medium-sized enterprises in cities, the number of employment opportunities decreases, which makes employment opportunities for a large surplus rural labor force going to cities also reduce. It has become another grim fact. The misguided reform process is very radical, which interferes with the normal order of socialist countries and is very destructive. It also confirms an old Chinese saying that the heart of Sima Zhao is well known to passers-by. Now, China must expose this evil to the world and let passers-by know it (Yang, 2016). The messy waves caused by the argument of the "pan-market" have led to some radical policies or practices, which have jeopardized the stable navigation of China's development. Therefore, to realize the great rejuvenation of the Chinese nation, China must firmly criticize the trend of "pan-marketization" in the theoretical and ideological field, eliminate the severe harm it has caused, and revise the radical reform policies and practices with the color of generalization. Only in this way can China turn the grand blueprint of the Chinese Dream into reality.

New Concept of Economic and Social Development Must be Condensed

The successful practice of China's reform and opening-up tells us that it is impossible to grasp the complexity of modern society by relying solely on economic analysis in a country with a large population and significant differences in regional conditions. In other words, pure marketization may not solve all the problems in modern society. The practices of adapting Western economic theories mechanically and the arguments that attempt to influence or even manipulate the reform process can only push out some practical radical methods under the label of deepening reform, the result of which is often to disturb the harmonious atmosphere of Chinese society. To lay a foundation for developing socialism with Chinese characteristics and building an innovative country, to rectify the chaos, to have a deeper understanding of the significance of creating an original state, to remove all obstacles to the realization of the Chinese dream, and to realize the grand vision of rejuvenation of the Chinese nation, innovative economic and social development concepts are needed to guide the construction of contemporary socialism and to establish or conform to the following development ideas:

Participate in international competition

Developing socialism with Chinese characteristics and building an innovative country is inevitable in Chinese history. On the one hand, China is thriving at this stage; on the other hand, it has indeed reached a very critical historical period. The country must redesign its strategic layout according to the changes in the international situation and the reality of the domestic social economy. Otherwise, it will lose a once-in-a-lifetime historical opportunity. China's global strategic issues are significant and should not be underestimated. Therefore, the connotation of "a Community of Shared Future for Mankind" conforms to the implication of national rejuvenation. The construction of the "Community of Shared Future for Mankind" is in line with the mode of world development, which has changed from focusing only on the realization of self-interest to the style of the win-win model. China has completed its preliminary industrialization and has developed at an alarming rate in some areas. The country is gradually equipped with the potential strength to become a world power. World history has repeatedly shown that the growth of an emerging power often means the decline of the hegemonic dominant country of the previous generation. However, based on the actual status of a socialist state, China has repeatedly declared and proved that China is on a path of peaceful development and will never seek dominance and hegemony. Building a Community of Shared Future for Mankind is China's plan for world development in the new era (Ren, 2018).

Since the resource space of the world market is limited, countries that want to be the world's hegemon will never allow China to become stronger gradually. A small part of people in these countries must desperately contain China and advocate the theory of China's rise as high power. Therefore, China should have its global strategic layout, and the critical point or value orientation of this strategic layout is to maximize China's national interests. On this issue, a national strategy for the new period is needed. Once having a correct national plan and implements it step by step, China will grow into a developed country with international competitiveness in 50 years to realize the dream of the great rejuvenation of the Chinese nation.

Therefore, the focus of the current work is, based on thoroughly criticizing the "pan Market" theory, to reaffirm the confidence of the socialist road with Chinese characteristics and enhance the country's innovative ability, adhere to the "one belt and one road" initiative and complement the structural reform of supply-side, to build a new era of the modern economic system effectively with more abundant and more impact potential energy of the comprehensive national strength and show the grandeur of a revitalized nation in the international arena of the 21st century. It is gratifying to note that the introduction of the Chinese dream is the crystallization of the wisdom of the whole nation centered on the leadership of the CPC Central Committee with Xi Jinping as the core. It is full of the philosophies of coordinated development and maintains the healthy thinking of developing socialism with Chinese characteristics. Through the supplement in the construction practice, it will inevitably lead to the development of the national economy into a new world (Xie & Xie, 2014).

Grasp the correct direction of developing a socialist market economy

Xi Jinping pointed out at the 40th anniversary of the reform and opening up that "we must unswervingly consolidate and develop the public sector of the economy, unswervingly encourage, support and guide the development of the non-public economy, give full play to the decisive role of the market in the allocation of resources, give better play to the role of the government, and stimulate the vitality of all types of market players." The core issue of the reform of the economic system is to deal with the relationship between government and the market. In contrast, the focus and difficulty of establishing the socialist market economy system reform will be the state-owned enterprises, which represents the process of separating the ownership of means and materials of production from that of products. After 40 years of reform and innovation, China's state-owned enterprises have established a modern enterprise system and gradually become the main body of the market. Insisting on autonomous change has laid a solid foundation for our country to become an innovative country.

Therefore, China should firmly keep to the top priority of economic development, stress that science and technology are the first productive force and produce high-tech and high value-added products so that it can participate more actively in international economic competition. According to statistics, China's gross domestic product increased from 367.9 billion yuan (about 214 billion US dollars) in 1978 to 82.7 trillion yuan (about 12.4 trillion US dollars) in 2017, with an average annual real growth rate of 9.5%, which is much higher than that of the world economy of 2.9% in the same period. China's share of the world's gross domestic product has risen to 15.2% from 1.8% at the beginning of the reform and opening, and it has contributed more than 30% to world economic growth. China's total import and export of goods increased from 20.6 billion US dollars to more than 4 trillion US dollars, with increasing use of foreign direct investment exceeding 2 trillion US dollars and a total amount of outbound investment reaching 1.9 trillion US dollars (Liu & Zhang, 2018) (See Figure 4.2 for details). The strategic goal of building an innovative country can be achieved by establishing a socialist market economic system, insisting on autonomous innovation and establishing famous commercial brands that can enjoy a global reputation.

However, the establishment of a socialist market economy system is by no means the mechanical "marketization" of the whole state. The social responsibility of an advanced political party must not be swept away by the trend of "pan-marketization." The substantive expression of market economic theory, in some respects, is purely technological, which has excellent limitations and cannot cover all social stuff. Therefore, China should criticize the trend of "pan-marketization." Only after erroneous statements have been dispelled, can the correct theories be established and developed. The goal of the socialist market economy is to ensure that the country is prosperous, and the people are well-off and healthy with better rights and interests, and that all Chinese people live in a safe and beautiful countryside.

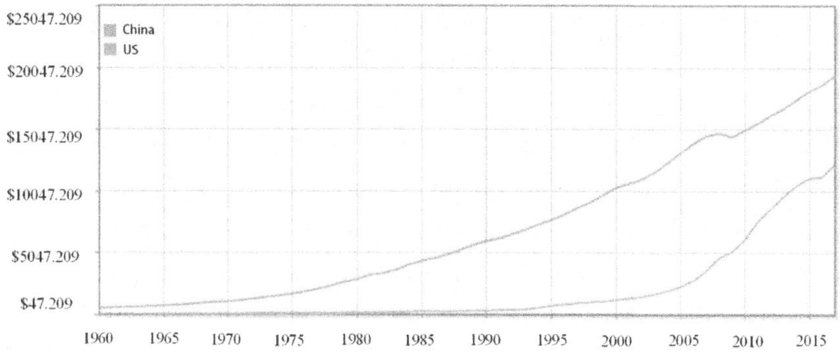

Figure 4.2 Gross Domestic Product between China and the United States from 1960 to 2018 (billion)

The words and deeds of Pan-marketization are misunderstandings of the market economy and distortions of market-oriented reform. One more step forward in truth is a fallacy, and turning marketization into "pan-marketization" is the first step towards delusion. Socialism with Chinese characteristics has entered a new era, and China's economic development has introduced a new era as well. It is necessary to continually improve the property rights system and market-oriented allocation of factors to achieve effective incentives for property rights and free flow of elements to solve the problems about the relationship between the government and the market and better play the role of the government. It is necessary to improve the management system of state-owned assets and consolidate the basic socialist economic system. It is required to deepen the reform of fiscal, taxation, and financial systems and enhance the ability of financial services to the real economy (Wang, 2019).

Maintaining the common interests of society

How to develop the socialist market economy with Chinese characteristics? There are a great many suggestions from Chinese scholars. The recognized core issue is how to carry out social change or social reconstruction. There are also many problems reflected in the process of the reform of the market economic system, among which there are two points to be pointed out. Firstly, the market economy is not equal to a market society. Former French Prime Minister Jospin has a famous saying: "market economy, not the market society" (Han, 2013). The market economy is indeed an effective economic system for allocating resources. However, its principles cannot wholly penetrate or dominate the whole social life. In recent years, the reforms in some fields have made frequent mistakes and even caused severe harm, such as the reform of the medical market and the reform of education industrialization, which to some extent, has a direct relationship with the "pan-marketization." Secondly, the socialist market economy needs to be based on the principle of public ownership and distribution according to work. Modern sociology tells us that any economic system is embedded in the social foundation, meaning that without a proper social foundation, it is difficult to operate normally even with a perfect market economy.

To build a perfect socialist market economy in China, on the one hand, they need to continually practice socialism with Chinese characteristics and combine it with the market economy to produce higher efficiency. On the other hand, they should avoid blindness, prevent and avoid systemic economic risks and crises when practicing socialism in the way of resource allocation of the market economy, and treat and use it from a rational perspective (Liu, 2012). China must put an end to capitalist exploitation and safeguard the common interests of the people, which are necessarily national interests. For this reason, Xi Jinping put forward the idea of building a win-win and the "Community of Shared Future for Mankind," which conforms to the world development mode, realizes the transformation from focusing on self-interest to win-win way, and is a correct understanding of the differences and interdependence of all countries in the world (Zhang, 2017). Building a Community of Shared Future for Mankind requires balancing the common interests of all countries in the world. Only by grasping the common interests can they understand socialism, grasp the common interests, grasp the ownership relationship and its structure as well as the distribution relationship and its structure, so that we cannot divorce from reality, nor lose direction, nor lag the times and beyond the stage. From building a Community with a Shared Future for Mankind and everyday interests, this book analyzes the relationship between public ownership, planned economy, and distribution according to work, which further deepens the understanding of Marx's socialist conception and the construction of the great Chinese dream of rejuvenation.

Excellent national culture is the soul of economic construction

The Chinese culture, which has continuously been refined and honed by the Chinese nation in its thousands of years of development, is an inexhaustible motive force for the Chinese nation to resist aggression and oppression and seek independence and prosperity since modern times. Although the history of the Chinese nation is full of changes, it has always been moving forward in a high-spirited manner because of its profound historical origin and deep cultural foundation, and the tremendous indomitable spirit of the Chinese people. During the period of the reform and opening, China has once imitated the market economy theory implemented by the western industrialized countries, whose technological analysis method is worth studying and drawing lessons from. The advanced concepts in the market economy theory should continue to develop and flourish. However, if they want to combine socialism with the stable market economy with Chinese characteristics and form a theoretical system of economics, they must have enough support such as logic self-consistency, science, specialty, concreteness, and accuracy. The Chinese people must have full cultural confidence to realize this grand systematic project. Cultural self-confidence is the most fundamental national self-confidence and an indispensable spiritual driving force for social progress. Cultural self-confidence has experienced the development of "three self-confidence" to "four self-confidence" since it was put forward. This is the more accurate capture of "Chinese self-confidence" by the Chinese Communist Party and the state, the requirement of exerting the unique charm of Chinese culture, and the perfect response to the export of strong Western cultures (Hu, 2017).

Since the reform and opening, the theory of the socialist market economy in China has been the development of Marxism. However, there are still many imperfections in this theory, which need to be adjusted more carefully. To proceed from China's actual situation, they should not mechanically quote some market economic theories that seem to have no flaws from theoretical or technical perspectives. Such practices neglect the critical element of "different national conditions" and put the construction of China's material civilization on a non-existent beach without seeking truth from facts. Therefore, starting from China's national conditions, taking China's political, economic, cultural and historical traditions as a reference, and aiming at solving the problems arising in the reform of the economic system, attention should be paid to the following points: firstly, measuring the degree of social development by GNP alone and assessing the people's living standards by GDP per capita will be divorced from the situation of China where there are relatively few resources and from the cultural traditions and national habits that have been formed since ancient times. This will encourage the so-called advanced consumption and credit consumption, which will lead to a vicious circle of consumption if lasted for a long time, and ultimately lead to the decline of people's actual consumption level. Secondly, the excessive emphasis on economic benefits will fundamentally neglect social equity, resulting in unfair distribution of social wealth, polarization, and gradual accumulation of dissatisfaction among the masses to varying degrees, and the goal of shared prosperity cannot be achieved. Thirdly, although people can realize that the development of material civilization is the basis of social progress and they consistently emphasize spiritual enlightenment, in real life they have not carried forward the unique culture of the Chinese nation but have paid too much attention to the material basis, leading to the result that many young people despise the rich cultural heritage handed down by the Chinese nation, lose their initiative to build a spiritual civilization and their senses of national confidence and pride (Guo, 2014).

One Belt One Road and Chinese Dream

The report of the Nineteenth National Congress of the Communist Party of China pointed out that Chinese people should persist in promoting the construction of a community of human destiny, which refers to considering the legitimate concerns of other countries in the pursuit of their interests and promoting joint development of all countries in search of their development. Human beings have only one earth in which all countries live, so China should advocate the consciousness of "Community of Human Destiny." The global value of the community of human destiny includes the interdependent concept of global power, the idea of common interests, the concept of sustainable development, and the idea of global governance. On March 11, 2018, the first session of the 13th National People's Congress adopted an amendment to the Constitution, amending the twelfth natural paragraph of the Preamble to the Constitution from "Developing diplomatic relations and economic and cultural exchanges with other countries" to "Developing diplomatic relations and economic and cultural exchanges with other countries, and promoting the construction of a community of human destiny."

The dreams of the Chinese people are closely linked with those of the peoples of other countries. The realization of the Chinese dream cannot be separated from a peaceful international environment and a stable international order. Under the condition of taking charge of both domestic and international situations, China must take the road of peaceful development as a whole, pursue the win-win strategy of opening up, adhere to the correct concept of justice and benefit, establish a new security concept of collective, comprehensive, cooperative and sustainable development, so that Chinese people can seek the development prospects of opening up, innovation, inclusiveness, and reciprocity to promote and integrate civilized exchanges, and to construct an ecological system that respects nature and green development. By doing so, China has always been a contributor to world peace, global expansion, and international order.

Constructing a community of human destiny is the right path that China has pointed out for the world. The community of human destiny refers to considering the legitimate concerns of other countries in the pursuit of national interests and promoting the joint development of all countries in the search for their development. In his first meeting with foreign leaders since assuming the post of General Secretary, Xi Jinping said that the international community has increasingly become a "community of destiny" that is a mixture of all people, and that no country can be immune from the complicated situation of the world economy and global issues. "Community of Destiny" is a new concept of human society that has been repeatedly emphasized by the Chinese government. In the White Paper of China's Peaceful Development in 2011, it is proposed that the new connotation of shared interests and shared values of humankind should be sought from a unique perspective of the "community of destiny."

On September 26, 2015, Chinese President Xi Jinping attended the United Nations Development Summit at the United Nations Headquarters in New York and delivered a famous speech entitled "Seeking Common Sustainable Development as a Win-win Partner for Cooperation." Xi emphasized that the post-2015 development agenda should be a new starting point from which all countries should strive to achieve joint development with each other. The international community should strengthen cooperation and strive to achieve win-win cooperation. China is ready to work with all relevant parties to advance the "One Belt and One Road" initiative, put into operation the Asian Infrastructure Investment Bank (AIIB) and the Brics New Development Bank (NDB) at an early stage, and contribute to the economic growth and improvement of people's livelihood in developing countries. On September 28, Xi Jinping attended the general debate of the 70th United Nations General Assembly at the United Nations Headquarters in New York and delivered a famous speech entitled "Building a Community of Human Destiny through Cooperation and Win-win New Partners" in which he pointed out that all states should inherit and carry forward the purposes and principles of the Charter of the United Nations to build new international relations with win-win cooperation as the core and build a community of human destiny.

The keywords of the community of human destiny are human beings, destiny, and community. Human nature means that all humans should transcend national identity and embody the responsibility of the world; destiny refers to the upgrading of cooperation and win-win, reflecting destiny and universal; community means to transcend the global village, establishing the sense of big family and sharing a collective identity. The core tenet of the Community of Destiny is that all countries should share the destiny of the world; all states should write international rules; all governments should govern global affairs, and all nations should share development achievements. So it has been echoed by many developed and developing countries.

On February 10, 2017, the 55th session of the United Nations Commission for Social Development unanimously adopted the resolution on the social dimension of the New Partnership for Africa's Development (NEPAD). The concept of "Constructing a Community of Human Destiny" was first incorporated into the United Nations resolution. On November 1 of the same year, the First Committee for Disarmament and International Security of the 72nd session of the General Assembly adopted two security resolutions, namely, "Further Practical Measures to Prevent an Arms Race in Outer Space" and "No First Placement of Weapons in Outer Space." The concept of "Constructing a Community of Human Destiny" was reintroduced in these two United Nations resolutions for the second time.

United Nations Secretary-General Guterres commented on this: "China has become an important pillar of multilateralism, and the purpose of our practice of multilateralism is to establish a community of human destiny." Peter Thomson, President of the 71st UN General Assembly, said, "For me, this is the only future of mankind on this planet."

Promoting the construction of "One Belt and One Road" will encourage the building of the community of human destiny. China has put forward the proposal of building the "One Belt and One Road" initiative, which is to promote the strategy of opening to the outside world and has effectively developed the construction of infrastructure projects, interconnection, and economic growth in the areas along the line. It is also significant innovations and practical actions that have promoted the in-depth development of South-South cooperation, striving to achieve common development goals, helping the opening, tolerance and balanced development of the world economy, and reinventing the world's political and economic order (Guangming Daily, 2015).

In the context of the "New Normal" for the world economy, the globe needs a world of healthy economic development and progress of human civilization. China and the rest of the world also need this destiny of humankind, a prosperous and peaceful world. Xi Jinping's initiative of "One Belt and One Road" is to realize this great dream. Therefore, openness, inclusiveness, and fairness are the indispensable elements to solve the development problems in the new healthy trend of the world economy. They are more a political concept and a more standard, fair, and reasonable contribution of China to promote global economic governance.

The core of the "One Belt and One Road" construction as a win-win situation is to promote balanced regional economic development and to create a Eurasian Economic green circle through the two trade corridors of land and sea. Viewing from the regional analysis of development, first, based on the achievements of the western expansion in China, the construction of "One Belt and One Road" can open China's west and Eastern regions and narrow the differences in regional development. Secondly, it can use the coastal economic prosperity circle to connect the sea corridor, and at the same time, use the western geographical advantages to penetrate the Eurasian continent, to realize the full opening pattern of domestic marine economy. From the perspective of development strategy, it can be noticed that China will share the advantages of capital, technology, and equipment with the rest of the world, and establish a trinity of interest community, responsibility community and destiny community in the world economic system which is under the political structure of the world.

Promoting the construction of "One Belt and One Road" will further deepen and widen reform and open to the outside world. Reform and opening is not only China's basic national policy but also the fundamental driving force for China's development. The direction of China's reform will not be reversed but continue to deepen. China's open doors will not be closed but open wider and wider. China will continue to increase improvement, expand opening, comprehensively promote the rule of law and build a socialist country ruled by law following the established deployment and rhythm. China insists on giving full play to the decisive role of the market in the allocation of resources, giving a better match to the part of the government, encouraging competition, and opposing monopoly.

Like other countries in the world, China has the right to choose its development path, including the economic model, according to its national conditions. As a developing country, China is not perfect, but it is willing to learn from exceptional experience through reform and opening and continuously improve its institutional mechanisms and policies. China will do its own thing well, firmly implement the strategy of innovation-driven development, speed up the construction of a modern economic system, and promote high-quality economic development. China is willing to share new opportunities for China's development with other countries in the world. China will implement a high-level policy to ensure the liberalization and facilitation of trade and investment; comprehensively implement the system of national treatment plus negative list management before access; substantially loosen the barriers of market entrance; expand the opening up of service industries; further, reduce tariffs; build a transparent, efficient and fair market environment; develop a higher level of an open economy; create a more attractive investment environment, and work with all the countries in the world to pursue progress and share common development and prosperity.

Promoting the construction of "One Belt and One Road" will promote beneficiaries and win-win cooperation mutually among developed and developing countries. Pushing forward the creation of "One Belt and One Road" will help China and the EU to speed up the negotiation of China-EU investment agreement and strive for it as early as possible and put the issue of China EU FTA on the list on this basis. China will accelerate the negotiation process of China-Japan-ROK FTA and promote the early conclusion of the "Comprehensive Regional Economic Partnership Agreement." China will further improve the "One Belt and One Road" international cooperation; adhere to the principle of co-construction and sharing; and strive to achieve policy communication, facilities interconnection, smooth trade, financial integration, and shared aspiration of the people to add new impetus to current development.

The idea of a community of destiny has inherited and carried forward the purposes and principles of the Charter of the United Nations. It is the core concept of the principle of co-operation, co-construction, and sharing of global governance. It has shaped the soul for the construction of "One Belt and One Road," removing the negative sense that "mankind has only one earth, and all countries live together in a world" but forming a definite sense of "fate connecting and sharing weal and woe," that is, not only at the material level, but also at the institutional level and spiritual level, should all human beings seek common ground while reserving differences, assimilate differences, and shape the new human identity of "you have me, and I have you." In this way, the human can create the world as a modern civilization of human beings for the public, which is a world in harmony. In a word, it is the common desire of people of all nationalities in the world to strive to build a community of human destiny and work together to make a better future.

Conclusion

To realize the great economic and social project of the Chinese Dream requires Chinese people to remove all obstacles on the way forward, innovate a new outlook of economic and social development, and adjust the strategic objectives and approaches of current economic and social development appropriately. In the final analysis, economic growth is to achieve the well-being and shared prosperity of the whole people. Therefore, China must put the material civilization and spiritual civilization in the right place: material civilization is the foundation of socialist economic construction, and spiritual civilization is the direction of socialist progress.

Only by their promoting each other can China achieve the goal of building a moderately prosperous society in an all-round way and realize the Chinese dream. All kinds of negative phenomena caused by the trend of Pan-market economy theory have made some people confused or even dissatisfied with the development of a market economy. In the analysis of the causes of such negative phenomena, scholars have made different interpretations. They believe that in the face of the "pan-market" problem in the development of market economy, the Chinese need to have a deeper understanding of the meaning of the theory of the socialist market economy and the specific content of the great strategic concept of realizing the Chinese dream.

For many specific problems in the reform, starting from the appropriate content, including whether some reform measures are biased towards individual interest groups or whether some slogans or incorrect values are propagandized, the Chinese need to seriously layout facts and rationalize instead of blindly following the crowd. Only such a severe approach can ensure that the process of marketization is "impartial" and that China will become a socialist country with characteristics of democracy, the rule of law, fairness and justice, vitality, stability and order, and harmony between man and nature.

While realizing the great social project of the Chinese Dream, China should consolidate the economic foundation and highlight the importance of national defense construction supported by high-tech means. Socialist modernization will not be realized without strong enemies outside the country and disunity inside. On the other hand, from the perspective of national social and economic development, China needs to establish a systematic theory of promoting innovative countries, firmly hold on to the center of economic construction, and combine the "one belt and one road" initiative with the structural reform of supply side to effectively build a modern economic system in the new era (Bao & Bi, 2016).

The Chinese government should take the adjustment of the balanced development of the national economy and society as the basis, take the creation of the fullest employment environment as the direction, and take the achievement of the universal compulsory education and social security as the stage goal, to ensure that the people can live a prosperous life and the country can be healthy and wealthy. When necessary adjustments are made to the mechanism or strategy of economic and social development, China must completely abandon the fallacy of "pan-marketization," which should be denied realistically; otherwise, the Chinese leadership cannot explain it to the people of the whole country. After these strategic adjustments are made, necessary reforms will be made to the existing administrative system, and adequate supervision mechanisms will be established to curb corruption at the management level from the source (Zhang, 2005).

From the perspective of development, China must renovate the concept of economic and social development, regard social equity and shared prosperity as the criteria for rebuilding Chinese social family and strive to build an innovative country aiming at realizing the "Community of Shared Future for Mankind" in the world, especially through the construction of "One Belt One Road," to enhance the realization of "Chinese Dream." Market economy theory needs to be enriched, which, however, must be re-interpreted and sublimated. In the fierce competition of comprehensive national strength, they have no other choices but to remove all obstacles that hinder the realization of the Chinese dream, overcome difficulties, and make the country better and more prosperous. Only in this way can they realize the grand goal of the collective planning of the national leadership, and finally make the great dream of national prosperity, national rejuvenation, and people's happiness come true.

Chapter 5
Environment Protection in the Strategy of One Belt and One Road

Notably, the implementation of One Belt One Road has been mainly focused on the economic level. However, if China put environmental protection in economic cooperation and economic development, the Chinese can better meet the significance of improving the quality of the economy. The economic development without environmental protection is doomed to be an extensive mode with high energy consumption and high pollution discharge, which will cause a large number of international disputes. To promote the implementation of the "One Belt and One Road" strategy, China must take the project's sustainability and environmental impact into account. Constructing the green one belt and one road are all of importance. This chapter analyzes the significance of environment protection in the "One Belt One Road strategy and presents the ideas of interaction environment protection and self-discipline environment protection and some policy suggestions.

Introduction

The interaction between human activities and the natural environment has been affecting the development of the world for a long time. With the social and economic development, this type of relevance has drowned more great concerns. Protecting the environment needs an innovative spirit and requires many proprietary technologies to create high-quality products in economically productive activities continuously. However, the development of history is twists and turns. Therefore, there is a lot of benefit game in environmental problems, and the Nash equilibrium usually exists in a variety of situations (Trejo, Clempner and Poznyak, 2017).

We apply the game theory to discuss the influence of the distribution of interests and the theoretical analysis of Nash equilibrium in detail. We then analyze some cases that cause environmental deterioration by pointing out some of China's domestic causes of such incidents, at the same time, the international market technology barriers, represented by the three E.U. directives, are mainly referred to. Finally, we propose some suggestions to solve the problems by stressing that China must continuously improve and formulate laws and regulations, correctly handle the disputes of interests among the state, enterprises, and individuals, and make unremitting efforts to protect the environment (Ceparano and Quartieri, 2017).

China's environmental protection is not only related to its domestic situation but also associated with international environmental protection; especially, it is related to the countries involved in the "One Belt One Road" initiatives. In the complicated international climate change negotiations, China must continue to negotiate within the framework of the UN and plays its role as a responsible vast country. In the development process of "One Belt One Road," adhere to environmental protection is a banner to establish a responsible big country image, and highlight the transformation of China's ecological civilization. The UN post-2015 plan covers 17 areas and 169 development goals, which are highly related to the theme of environmental protection. Whether it is infrastructure or international production capacity cooperation, environmental protection should be put forward first. One belt, one road and one green road, will not only help promote the implementation of the strategy but also help to enhance the soft power of China's development path and ecological civilization concept internationally.

Activities for Environmental Protection

The inherited, conservative thought flutters around because of the long-term existence of the traditional large-scale machine production mode. Plundering resources in pursuit of self-interest and sacrificing the environment in pursuit of profits, these economic behaviors mentioned above can be seen everywhere in the real world. As a result, the ecological situation has been deteriorating in the world, and then the development of human civilization is facing a great crisis. How to break this vicious cycle of a tough situation? The first prerequisite is innovation. Admittedly, change is challenging with a grinding and tortuous process (Zhang, 2013).

In the long history of China, innovation is the power source of social progress, and the change represented by the four great inventions in Chinese feudal society not only benefits the Chinese nation but also benefits all humankind. Innovation is the power source of social progress. The giant, Marx, praised the significant changes of the gunpowder, the compass, the printing, and so on, that they opened a new era of human society. He said: gunpowder, the compass, printing — these are the three great inventions to predict the arrival of the bourgeois society. Gunpowder smashed the honor; the compass opened the world market and established colonies, and printing became a Protestant tool. In general, it becomes the means of scientific rejuvenation and becomes the most powerful lever to create the necessary premise for the development of the spirit (Max, 1979). Gunpowder, the compass, printing, and papermaking are four great inventions of ancient China. They have a profound influence on the world after they have been abroad. The four great designs mainly played a crucial role in promoting the progress of the European Renaissance. These advances include the fields of science culture, production technology, and social politics.

After the establishment of The People's Republic of China, primarily since the reform and opening-up, the innovation has been strongly supported by the governments at all levels. Deng Xiaoping attached foremost importance to the scientific theory and technological transformation, considering it the only way to improve social productivity. Deng pointed out: introducing technology to transform Enterprises, the first to learn, second to promote innovation (Deng, 1994). How to master modern technology and improve production efficiency? Deng clearly said: to master advanced technology, to be good at learning, but also to be good at innovation. Under the guidance of innovative ideas, the national innovation activities have been flourishing for decades.

First, there is a significant increase in the number of scientific research institutions and patent applications. The implementation of innovation activities needs a material basis. In the social and economic life, the scientific research institution is the base of innovation, and the invention patent is the typical innovation result. During the period of years 2000 to 2010 for the implementation of two five-year programs, the quantity of innovation base and the amount of patent application in China have significantly increased. Until 2010, the state established 127 National Engineering Research Centers based on industrial enterprises and set up 729 state-level enterprise technology centers. It was two times as much as the initial period of the"11th Five-Year." Five thousand five hundred thirty-two provincial enterprise technology centers were established, compared with the year of 2007, increasing more than 1500.

The state-sponsored enterprise technology center in 2010 spent more than 180 billion yuan on R & D investment, which is 4.2 times than that in the early "11th Five-Year." According to the same caliber, the average annual growth rate increased by 21.4% over the five years, the scientific and technological personnel of large and medium-sized industrial enterprises reached 2468.2 thousand, accounting for 5.19% of the employees (Zhang, 2017).

The national patent application volume has a blowout. This blowout is the outcome of the establishment of many scientific and technological research centers at all levels and the increase in the numbers of scientific and technical personnel and business organizations. Statistics show that during the "11th Five-Year" period, China's patent applications increased rapidly, of which 1451 thousand invention patents were applied, which are 2.6 times of the "10th Five-Year" period. In 2010, there were more than 391 thousand patent applications for inventions, the second largest in the world. During the "11th Five-Year" period, the patent applications of utility models and designs in China were 1289 thousand and 1554 thousand, respectively, which is 2.4 times and 3.1 times that of the "10th Five-Year," keeping the number one in the world. During the "11th Five-Year" period, the State Intellectual Property Office granted 50 gold awards for Chinese patents, including 5 Chinese design gold awards, and 525 outstanding Chinese patent awards, including 32 Chinese Design Excellence Awards. With the support of patent technology, the national economy has developed rapidly, and the people enjoy a large quantity of high quality and green products, and the living standard has been improved (Wang and Tian, 2012).

Second, the number of international patent applications in the world ranks first in the world. China's innovation activities cross national boundaries and move towards the world. The international patent application submitted by the worldwide recognized Patent Cooperation Treaty (PCT) reflects the innovation ability of a country, a region, or an enterprise, showing the technological value and market value of the innovators. The statistics released by the World Intellectual Property Organization (WIPO) on March 6, 2012, showed that China's PCT international patent application increased significantly from 2009. It has been ranked first in the world for three consecutive years. China's PCT global patent application growth rate was up to 33.4% in 2011, 12 percentage points higher than that of Japan, which was second in the year. In 2004, China's PCT international patent application volume was 1706, ranking the top 10 in the world. In 2011, China's PCT global patent application volume was 16406 and entered the fourth place in the world. In 2011, the profound impact of the international fiscal crisis, which originated in the US Wall Street, continued to emerge. The European sovereign debt crisis was fermented continuously, and the economic development of western developed countries such as North America and Europe were facing difficulties. In contrast, the emerging countries had significant growth. The development trend of the world economy was reflected in the change of PCT international patent application (Zhang, Nong, and Han, 2017).

Third, there are great achievements in scientific and technological innovation of environmental protection. Innovative performance is very prominent in the field of environmental protection, and the outstanding results of science and technology are continually emerging. Whether intellectual property creation, environmental science basic research and management technology creation or energy-saving and emission reduction, water pollution control, and air pollution control, many research achievements have emerged. Statistics show that in the period of "11th Five-Year," 227 performances in the national environmental protection science and technology achievements were awarded at the national level.

Among them, there were 36 scientific and technological achievements in 2006, 41 awards in 2007, 48 honors in 2008, 62 awards in 2009, and 40 awards in 2010. Among the awards, there are 21 first prizes, 78-second prizes, and 128 third prizes. These awards are given to the scientists who work in the field of water, air, soil, solid waste, noise, ecology, rural areas, nuclear radiation, and environmental emergency, environmental monitoring, environmental information systems, ecological risk assessment. These technological innovation projects have both the achievements of significant scientific research programs for the joint research on watersheds and critical environmental issues in the region, as well as the completion of enterprises in independent innovation to solve specific technical problems; both the direct service for environmental management systems, technical regulations and standards of research results, but also the critical technology, critical equipment, and complete equipment of "controlling source reduction" (Wang and Tian, 2012).

Scientists in West China have worked hard to overcome the difficulties, and many award-winning technical achievements came to the fore. For example, "Research and application of a new generation of integrated oxidation ditch wastewater treatment technology in small towns of Guizhou province" project have designed a new sewage treatment facility, adjusted the operation parameters, and improved the sewage treatment efficiency. As another example, research and demonstration project of sewage treatment technology and reuse technology in high and cold areas project, it has constructed a cold-resistant microbial community system (Hou, 2017). Under low temperature, it can still guarantee the quality of effluent reaches the first level A standard. Compared with similar technologies, the land area can be reduced by 30%, the investment can be saved by 25%, and the running cost can be reduced by 20%. The last case, "Study on the risk and Countermeasures of water pollution events in China's transboundary river" project, established a multi-objective decision making computer model and standardized input benefit evaluation system. It proposed a risk analysis method for cross-boundary river pollution events, which laid a methodological foundation for China's environmental foreign policy and strategy research (Zhao and Ren, 2012). These award-winning projects have achieved remarkable results. They have made outstanding contributions to solving major environmental problems and raising the level of environmental management and environmental science and technology.

Marx said that science and technology are productive forces. Facts have proved that these words are right. Science and technology are primary productive forces (Deng, 1993). The benefits of environmental protection science and technology and their award-winning technological achievements are apparent, and these facts fully demonstrate this glorious conclusion. To achieve the goal of building an environment-friendly society, China must continue to vigorously develop science and technology on environmental protection in the future (Li, 2017).

After the establishment of The People's Republic of China, it has been the direction for people in all walks of life in the country to change the country's inheritance for thousands of years of the small-scale peasant economy and to build a modern, industrialized nation, and remarkable achievements have been made. After a long period of studies, some scholars of the Chinese Academy of Social Sciences evaluated some comprehensive indicators and found that after the implementation of the "10th Five-year" plan, the level of China's industrialization development belonged to the second half of the mid-industrialization period or the period of a high degree of industrialization in the period of heavy-chemical industrialization (Chen et al., 2007).

In the latter half of the implementation of the "11th Five-Year" Plan, the composite index of China's industrial modernization level exceeded 36.7, which means that the overall level of China's industrial modernization has surpassed 1/3 of the world's most advanced level, in other words, 1/3 of the way has passed in the country's modern industrialization (Chen, 2009). However, many scholars in the world think that based on the historical experience of some industrialized countries, there will be many difficulties in industrialization and development after this stage, and the process will be even more arduous. There are many reasons for these difficulties, including objective reasons as well as subjective reasons (Liu, 2017).

Although rich in natural resources and abundant labor resources, China is also a vast country with a relatively low per capita natural resource ownership. China's total water resources account for 7% of the world's complete water resources, ranking sixth. But only 2400 m3 per capita, accounting for 25% of the world's per capita water consumption, ranking the 119th in the world and one of the 13 water-deficit countries in the world. Due to the demographic factors, the per capita arable land and grassland resources in China are 1/3 of the world average; per capita, forest resources are 1/5 of the world average. Because of the historical legacy of the irrational economic structure and management system imperfections, there is a weakness in China's industrialization with a low level of technology and a mismatch in its structural mix. They inevitably lead to low efficiency, resource depletion, and environmental damage. Because such structural and technological maladjustment may lead to increased consumption in production, or a large backlog of products, or idle production equipment, resulting in a direct waste of resources (Gao, 2016).

In contrast, the overall utilization rate of mineral and water resources in China is only about 25% of the overall utilization rate of developed countries. The consumption intensity of iron, wood, and cement is 3 to 5 times, 4 to 7 times, and eight times in developed countries, respectively. The depletion rate of China's massive mineral reserves is much larger than the annual growth rate of reserves, and the production reserves of production mines are depleting (Du, 2011).

The production of 2/3 of the significant non-ferrous metal mines in China reaches the middle and late stages, making the scale of mining development and production capacity are severely restricted. China's per capita relative share of resources is low. Its consumption intensity is high; its management philosophy and methods are obsolete and backward. The result is that the losses caused by the damage to ecology and the environment in the construction of the whole country are huge, and the amount calculated in terms of value amounts to an astonishing amount. The proportion of its share of gross domestic product at the beginning of this century exceeded 9%. Pollution has been paid or will have to pay when considering the intangible loss of environmental resources. From the perspective of environmental and resource economics, economic growth may even be called negative growth in some respects (Geng, 2017).

In recent years, with the increasing environmental problems and the improvement of people's awareness of environmental protection, the issue of environmental pollution has not only become a critical restriction factor for the industrialization of the country. Still, it has also become a new inducement for mass incidents. There were incomplete statistical data on the situation of environmental disputes throughout the country from 1995 to 2006. The total number of letters from the masses in 1995 was 58678. The total number of letters from the masses reached 616122 in 2006. The number of environmental letters and visits has increased by ten times over the past 11 years (Yang, 2008). Some of the letters and visits have not been adequately solved, and some of them are converted into group events. In August 2009, a lead and zinc metallurgy enterprises in Changqing Town, Fengxiang County, Shaanxi Province, named Shaanxi Dongling Smelting Company, had long-term lead emissions exceeding safety standards, which has led to environmental pollution disaster. The company's violation led 615 of the 731 children to have blood lead over the norm in the surrounding Mao Daokou

Village and Sun Jia Nantou Village of Changqing. After a definitive test, a total of 851 children under the age of 14 were found to have excessive levels of lead in their blood. One hundred seventy-four children with blood lead levels exceeding 250 micrograms per liter were moderate to severe lead poisoning (Bai and Zhang, 2017).

On the morning of August 16, 2009, hundreds of angry villagers near Dongling Smelting Co. hit the Dongling Plantation. This factory exclusive railway line of nearly three hundred meters fence was overturned; the windshields of the more than ten large trucks and engineering cars (used to send coal to the province) were smashed! Hundreds of local police were stationed in the incident area to maintain order (Xinhua net, 2009). After the incident, the government of Shaanxi province, Baoji city and Fengxiang county, and the Dongling company took active treatment and economic compensation for sick children. It also invested 300 million yuan and implemented a whole off-site relocation project for 425 villagers in the lead threat area. The villagers were relocated to the safety zone 1350 meters away from the enterprise. This incident is not without warning. In fact, before the children's lead poisoning broke out, the villagers in Changqing Town had already had clashes with the local administrative authorities and the Dongling Smelting Company for several times. Still, in the end, because the company can pay huge profits, the problem was always brought to a dead end. It is typical, and people criticized for unscrupulous behavior (Dong, 2010).

The problem of environmental pollution in China is not only disturbed by the process of industrialization, but also criticized by China's domestic public opinion, and it also affects China's international image. Organization for Economic Co-operation and Development (OECD) is an intergovernmental international economic organization consisting of 34 market economy countries. In a 2007 published report, the organization said, "China's economy is rapidly approaching to the developed countries, but the environmental level is like the poorest countries in the world." In 2009, the American Forbes magazine once published a report on the issue of the People of China are Difficult to Allow Children to be polluted. The article stated: China has become a world factory, but many places have not implemented environmental protection measures. The result is that the rural pollution near the coal factory is severe, and a layer of dust will be covered on the newly parked car windshield. Many rivers in China are also polluted, no longer suitable for industrial use, not to mention being used as a drinking water (He and Chen, 2012).

The media in Japan, South Korea, and other countries often take the issue of China's environmental pollution and are trying to shape China into a dirty neighbor. It seems to some people in these countries that the dust storms in China have crossed the sea to Korea and Japan. Some foreigners concern that if China will be drowned by its wastewater before becoming a stronger economy in the world? The Chinese must have an appropriate attitude to these indecent and biased foreign opinions.

On the one hand, face the question candid; on the other hand, express their views clearly. The dangerous environmental pollution in China is a fact, but some foreign enterprises in China can't escape. For example, a lot of Japanese enterprises only do some low-pollution and high-added value businesses after the end of product design and production, and the middle pollution links are set up in China. Many European and North American countries have already transferred certain high-pollution and high-emission products to China. Some of these objectively formed a situation where China is assuming environmental responsibilities (Mu, 2013).

In brief, China's environmental situation is a mixed development during the implementation of the "11th Five-Year" Plan. The exciting new highlights from China are: energy conservation and emission reduction have achieved initial success; emission of pollutants has dropped for the first time; Beijing's green Olympic construction has achieved its stated goals. Of course, some environmental phenomena are worrying. For example, water is the source of life. However, the data released by the Ministry of Environmental Protection (MEP), National Development and Reform Commission (NDRC), Ministry of

Finance (MOF), and Ministry of Water Resources (MWR) indicates that China's water environment is still not optimistic until 2010. Liaohe River and the middle and upper reaches of the Yellow River are heavily polluted, and the river, the lake around the lake in Haihe, Chaohu, and Dianchi has severe pollution.

According to some scholars' analysis, taking the outbreak of cyanobacteria pollution in Taihu Lake in Jiangsu Province as a landmark in 2007, it shows that the pollution of rivers and lakes in China has reached a dangerous critical point, subverting the previous development model of pursuing GDP growth at the expense of the environment, involving environmental issues the number of mass incidents has increased. The reason for this is that the lagging traditional economic development model still has strong negative inertia. The special interest groups formed by some local selfishness are selfishly self-reliant. They continue to plunder their natural resources because they are unwilling to renounce their benefits (Friends of Nature and Yang, 2008). In short, the environment in China still has not gotten rid of the crises. Some deep-rooted contradictions have continuously been out breaking. The environment protection cause has been struggling with the transformation, and the tension in the exciting game has been disrupted. In-depth study of multi-stakeholder games around environmental issues and identify the crux of the problem, which will be very conducive to the protection of the environment, and improve the speed of construction and development (Peng, 2017).

Causes of the Deterioration

China's industrialization has just finished 1/3 of the journey. The overall level is still relatively backward. At the same time, it is also limited by the un-emancipation of thought and understanding, and the national economic construction has taken some twists and turns in its development. Besides, competition in the international market economy is very fierce. Some industrialized countries are double-faced for the sake of their interests. Some foreign and domestic factors are often intertwined, forming some adverse effects. The construction of China's coke production and export trade twists and turns, along with other product exports, encountered technical barriers, which is a typical example Trade profitability and environmental degradation, the current performance of this contradiction is very prominent, indicating that the Chinese industry must aim in the correct direction, promptly correct some of the mistakes for sustainable development (Sheng, 2017).

China is a developing country with a low level of industrialization. Its production and export trade of many products is at a low level. This is an unavoidable historical stage in the growth of a country. However, it is not easy to go through this initial stage. Mainly, due to the complicated and fierce political and economic competition in the international community, the Chinese people have encountered many severe challenges in the process of progress (Zhang, 2017).

Firstly, the evil consequence of forgetting honor at the prospect of profits. Any countries in the initial stages of industrialization, the products produced are not high-end level; they all have to provide low-end products. In the early twenty-first Century, China used to create a large amount of coke for export trade and the accumulation of funds. In 1985, China exported over 6 million tons of coke. In 2003, the country's coke production reached 178 million tons, and the export volume was 13 million tons. China has become the world's largest producer and exporter of coke, accounting for 45% of the world's total output and 60% of world trade. Coke production has brought good profits to China. Since 2003, the domestic market price of coke rose from 300 yuan per ton to 1,300 yuan per ton (Zeng and Sun, 2011).

Similarly, affected by the supply-demand relationship, coke prices in the international market soared from an average of about 200 dollars per ton in 2003 to more than 400 dollars per ton in the first quarter of 2004. In a period, this market price and profit index have a strong inducement. Therefore, to obtain high profits, some enterprises blindly expand production and blindly invest in the construction of coking projects, which leads to serious duplication of investment. Some unapproved, private coking projects are everywhere. In 2003, Chinese coke production was 180 million tons, and the output of coke exceeded

200 million tons in 2004. A lot of money continues to enter the coking industry. In 2005, there were about more than 700 large-scale coking enterprises in China, including more than 1900 large and medium-sized coke oven, among them, the output of small technology of "small coke oven" was about 40million tons (Wang and Mao, 2011).

As the price of coke continues to rise, the production of small soil coke with no pollution treatment measures continues to increase, and Chinese coke production capacity is increasing. At the end of 2005, the annual production and sales of coke in China were about 3 million tons, and the production capacity exceeded 4 million tons, and the production capacity was severe overcapacity. With the rapid development of the coke industry, coke oven capacity expands rapidly, and the coking industry is not healthy and super high-speed growth. There is only one reason that the coke price is high (Dong, 2010).

Secondly, the "two high and one resources" industry create severe pollution. Coking is a typical "two highs and one resource" industry with high energy consumption, high pollution, and resources-oriented. In China, the level of coking technology and equipment is less than that of developed countries, and the processing and utilization of coking by-products are backward. Thus severe pollution has been formed. Under the existing conditions in China, 1 ton of coke is made of 2 tons of coal, which consumes a large amount of energy. According to the test, the production of 1 ton of Coke will produce about 400m^3 gases. In the process of coking, a significant quantity of dust, carbon monoxide, and toxic gases will be discharged into the atmosphere, containing a variety of substances that would cause cancer or deformity. The tar and wastewater removed from the coking unit also include a large number of toxic substances, which will pollute the groundwater for a long time after infiltration into the ground. However, to gain profit, many soil coke ovens make production continuously. These small soil coke production technologies are backward. They cause considerable waste of resources and environmental pollution (Gao, 2016).

Taking Shanxi province as an example, in early 2006 of "11th Five-Year," 92.02 million tons of coke was produced in the area, accounting for 33% of the country's output. Shanxi province has 13.30 million tons of coke from its own-export and export-trade, accounting for 89.8% of China's coke trade volume, accounting for 40.5% of the world's coke trade. However, the coking industry is typical high pollution and high consumption industry. The coking process will produce a lot of waste gas, wastewater, and solid waste. It is one of the most polluting industries (Sheng, 2017).

In September 2006, the former State Environmental Protection Administration announced that the air quality of 43 cities in the country was inferior to the third standard, of which the Shanxi province accounted for 16. Shanxi coking industry on the air and water pollution load accounted for the province's total pollution load of 40% and 30%. Inferior class V water accounted for more than 70%, much higher than the national average of 44%. The coke industry has brought economic benefits to Shanxi, as well as resource consumption and environmental pollution. Shanxi is the largest province of coke production and the most polluted Province in China. As the former granary of Shanxi Fence Valley, due to the backward operation of coke production mode, especially the operation mode of small coke and improved coke, the result is that black smoke billows in the area, air pollution is severe, water pollution is dangerous, and farmland can be cultivated less and less. In a period, there are many areas with severe air pollution in Shanxi province. Under the condition of no wind or breeze, the state of the sky is dim, and the smell is smoky. It has a severe impact on the ecological environment and the physical and mental health of the local people (Li, 2017).

Thirdly, it is essential to recognize the essence of trade disputes. In sharp contrast, the western developed countries, to protect their environment, reduce coke output and even ignore the development of the domestic iron and steel industry, and close a lot of coking plants. It is reported that from 1996 to 2000, the production of coke was reduced by 10.17% in the United States, 9.9% in Japan in the same period, 7% in Germany, and 18.3% in Britain. Australia is a resource-rich country of iron ore and coking coal. Because of environmental cost considerations, Australia does not develop iron and steel industry and coke industry, but only exports iron ore and coking coal (Wang and Tian, 2012).

From 1998 to 2004, the entire world has closed plants with the production capacity of nearly 18 million tons of coke, and most of them were in Europe and the United States. Due to the closure of many backward coking coal production plants in the European countries, the local coke production capacity is further shrinking. The coke resources necessary for the development of iron and steel enterprises are heavily dependent on Chinese export. Such things appear more in the European Union (EU). In 2003, the European Union imported about 4.4million tons of coking coal from China, accounting for 31% of the annual consumption of coke in the EU's steel industry (Liu and Liu, 2017).

The developed countries shut down their coking plants, but they transferred coke production and pollution load to China. That is why the EU has made a 180-degree turn in the attitude of China's coke exports. In 2003, the European Union also listed imported coke from China as an antidumping product and levied an anti-dumping duty of 32.6 euros per ton. Times change, at the beginning of 2004, the relevant departments of China proposed that the export quota of Coke will be reduced by 3 million tons in that year. On May 7, 2004, the EU threatened to appeal to WTO for China's action to restrict the export of coking coal.

On June 23, 2009, the United States and the European Union put forward a trade dispute request to China in the WTO framework, accusing China of 9 kinds of raw materials export violation. China repeatedly stressed that the quota system is the need to protect the use of natural resources and the environment. Unfortunately, on July 5, 2011, the WTO still ruled "China's violation." Subsequently, China appealed the result of the preliminary ruling. However, the Panel of Experts on WTO appeals maintained the core of the initial decision that China's export tax and quota on various industrial raw materials violated the WTO rules and rejected the calls filed by China on the preliminary ruling based on environmental protection or supply shortage. On January 30, 2012, the WTO ruled again on China's restriction on the export of nine raw materials: maintaining the core penalty of the preliminary ruling in July 2011, confirming that China's export tax and export quotas on raw materials for the steel and chemical industry run counter to the rules of international trade and must be corrected (Securities Daily, 2012).

The ins and outs of things are clear. On the one hand, China was constrained by the historical stage of its development and had to produce "two highs and one resources" products. On the other hand, when the production of these products was diminished, it immediately brought unwarranted accusations from the industrialized countries. On the contrary, some industrialized countries have used historical opportunities and technological advantages to stop or transfer highly polluting products, letting developing countries produce such low-end products, and they consume at high-end. "Behind will be attacked," which is a popular expression, but also a profound truth. Chinese people should maintain their usual attitude and catch up with each other and rise peacefully (Zhang, 2017). The experience of coke production and export is only a tribulation encountered by the Chinese people in the construction. In the high-tech era, there are still more difficulties in breaking through.

Firstly, it is important to realize the significance of technical standards. The low-carbon economy is the general trend of development in today's world and is also a place where market competition is very fierce. Environmental factors are outstanding in the field of the low-carbon economy. As a result, China faces more challenges in its development. Some scholars have shown that to transit the traditional economy to a low-carbon economy, to achieve the desired goal of success, it requires 62 kinds of critical technical expertise and universal technology support. Mainly due to historical reasons, among the 42 crucial technologies among them, China currently does not have the core technology. For example, relevant experts estimate that China's current energy efficiency is only 33%, about ten percentage points less than that of the advanced international level (Du, 2011).

China's higher energy consumption per unit product of 8 primary energy-consuming industries, such as electric power, iron, and steel, non-ferrous metal, and petrochemical, is higher than the advanced world level by more than 40%. The reason that led to this situation is that some key core technologies are not mastered. The difficulties encountered in the production and export of coke is the lag of technology and management. For example, the level of technical equipment is not high, the production process is backward, and environmental protection is not well managed, and so on. In the most basic measure of the quality of the product, there is still a defect in management and technology. For example, the foundation of standardization work in China is still weak and lags at the advanced international level. These include the low overall standards, the slow development speed, the lack of high-tech standards, the unsafe safety standards system, and the lag in resource conservation standards, which have become inaccessible to the national economic and social development requirements. Facing difficult international and domestic situation, it has become a very urgent task to speed up the development of standardization (Geng, 2017).

Secondly, there are new standards for three challenging instructions. The criteria for measuring things and their formulation seem simple, but they are not. During the period of China's "11th Five-Year," the European Parliament and the Council of Ministers of the European Union adopted three instructions with environmental protection contents and affecting international trade, commonly known as ecological protection directives. After these standards were put forward, some manufacturing enterprises in China immediately placed themselves at serious challenges. Waste Electrical and Electronic Equipment (2002/96/EC, WEEE) came into force on August 13, 2005. The core content of the WEEE instruction is that the manufacturer of electronic and electrical equipment circulated in the EU market must be legally responsible for the cost of reclaiming waste products (Mu, 2013).

The Restriction of the Use of Certain Hazardous Substances in Electrical and Electronic Equipment (2002/95/EC), abbreviated as "Restriction of Hazardous Substances (RoHS)." It came into force on July 1, 2006. The core content of the RoHS directive is that the contents of 6 substances in the new electronic devices which are put into the EU market must not exceed the standard. They are four kinds of heavy metals, namely, lead, cadmium, mercury, two types of bromine flame retardants with polybrominated two benzyl ether (PBDE), and polybrominated biphenyl (PBB).

The WEEE and RoHS instructions put forward high environmental standards for mechanical and electrical products. The EU market prohibits the entry of standard products. China's mechanical and electrical export enterprises have suffered a great deal of impact, and they have reached thousands of enterprises and about 200000 kinds of products. The product, which was affected by the directive, accounted for 71% of the electromechanical products exported to the European Union, with a total value of about $37 billion (Li, 2017).

The Framework for the Setting of Eco-design Requirements for Energy-using Products and Amending Council Directive (92/42/EEC) was approved by the European Parliament and the Council in 2005 (2005/32/EC), which is abbreviated as "Energy-using Products (EuP)," and entered into force on August 11, 2005. Before August 11, 2007, the EU completed the necessary steps to comply with this directive of the domestic legislation and administrative regulations, formally converted to EU laws and enforcement. The EuP directive has a significant impact on the export of Chinese household appliances. The initial calculation has brought about 50-billion-yuan loss to the Chinese household appliance industry.

The 25 European Union countries have successively implemented these three directives. They have formed the technical barriers (or it's called a green barrier, GBs) to international trade to the vast number of developing countries, including China (Duan, 2007). The green barriers made by the three orders still exist and produce a chain reaction beyond the European Union, which has a significant impact on the export of Chinese mechanical and electrical products.

Realize the Harmony between Human and Nature

At present, humankind has entered the fastest and most promising development stage in history. There are miraculous changes in science and technology and management. Countless things that are regarded as dreams become ordinary things today. It is the most important and close to the real work to deal with the shortcomings that still exist now and move forward to a better future.

No matter the difficulties encountered in the production or export of coke, or the challenges posed by the new EU directive, they all need to be dealt with scientifically and rigorously. We cannot only see the side of green barriers. Still, we cannot understand their rationality, which will directly impede the decision and lead to the failure to overcome the challenges. As a traditional Chinese saying goes, if you know your enemies and know yourself, you will not be imperiled in a hundred battles (Wang and Tian, 2012).

Firstly, China needs to understand scientific research and test results. On December 27, 2006, the European Parliament and the EU Council of Ministers jointly issued the "Directive on the Restriction of the Sales and Use of Perfluoro Octane Sulfonate" (2006/122/EC). The directive is the 30th revision of the Council on "the Directive on Harmonization of the Laws and Regulations of the Member States Concerning the Restriction on the Sales and Use of Dangerous Substances and Products Prohibited" (76/769/EEC). The EU issued the 2006/122/EC directive, not a contingency event, but a process of scientific inspection, production practice and life consumption, and a legal severe review procedure (Peng, 2017).

PFOS is an organic compound with characteristics of oil repellent, hydrophobic, and very stable chemical properties. It is widely used in various fields. In surface treatment, it can be applied to materials such as carpet, clothing, leather, textiles, and interior decoration, and so on. In the field of paper protection, it is used for contact with food, non-food contact, etc. Besides, in the industrial cleaning agent, foam fire, petrochemical industry, surfactant, metal plating inhibiting acid fog agent, photolithography, hydraulic oil, floor polishes, shampoo, coatings, pesticides, and other products, will also use the material (Zhang, Nong, and Han, 2017).

However, studies have shown that PFOS is one of the most challenging organic pollutants found in the world, and has high bioaccumulation, multiple-toxicity, and the capability of remote environment transmission. According to the hazard assessment results of the Organization for international economic cooperation and development (OECD), once organisms absorb PFOS, it will mainly distribute in blood and liver, and it is difficult to decompose through the metabolism of the plant. It takes 8.7 years in the half discharge time of the human body. Staff from the UK Department of Environment, Food and Rural Affairs (DEFRA) sent an independent assessment of PFOS for PBT (an abbreviation of "persistent, bioaccumulation and toxic"). The result is consistent with the OECD assessment and confirms that it will result in a risk of R48 (an abbreviation of Risk Phrases) in toxicological studies. In other words, prolonged exposure to PFOS, human health will be severely injured (Dong, 2010).

Secondly, China needs to have a deep understanding of the review of legal procedures. In December 2002, the Organization for Economic Co-operation and Development (OECD), held the thirty-fourth joint meeting of the chemical Committee. The conference defined PFOS as a substance that persists in the environment has biological savings and is harmful to human beings. According to the "Regulations on Assessment and Control of Existing Material Hazards," approved by Council of European Union (CEU) NO.793/93, Britain submitted the PFOS risk assessment report and the strategy of reducing PFOS hazards and the impact assessment of the approach to the European Commission.

The Scientific Committee on Health and Environmental Risks (SCHER) conducted a scientific review of the strategy submitted by the United Kingdom and confirmed the harmfulness of PFOS on March 18, 2005. On December 5, 2005, the European Commission, the only

European Commission that had the right to draft decrees, proposed a motion, formulating the draft proposals and instructions for limiting the sale and use of PFOS, and evaluating the cost, benefit, balance and legality of the project. On October 30, 2006, the European Parliament, the lower house of the two legislative assemblies of the European Union, voted in 632 votes to 10 for the first reading of the draft. On December 12, 2006, the draft directive was finally approved by the Council of ministers. On December 27, 2006, the instruction was officially announced and worked at the same time (He and Chen, 2012).

Other countries have also enacted laws that strictly prohibit the restriction of the proportion of such compounds in products. For example, in early 2007, Environment Canada released a regulatory proposal on PFOS and its salts and certain other compounds that prohibit the production, use, sale, and import of any PFOS-containing substance or product containing such material (Except for a small amount of exemption). The proposal was adopted in 2008, and the relevant provisions were written into the "Canadian Environmental Protection Act 1999" and came into effect on May 29, 2008. It is facing practical problems that put forward feasible solutions, which is the correct way to promote the joint development of environmental protection and economical construction.

The Chinese government must firmly implement the national legal system to protect the environment while promoting the "One Belt One Road" construction process. It must conscientiously enforce the domestic legal policy, eliminate backward production capacity, and protect the environment. It is necessary to perform further the "Notice of the State Council on Further Strengthening the work of eliminating backward production capacity (NO.7 document of State Council, 2010) and exerting the fundamental role in the allocation of resources by administrative means, applying the restraining function of laws and regulations and the threshold function of technical standards, eliminating the backward production capacity of coal, steel, cement, coke, paper making, and printing and dyeing industries (Hou, 2017).

The Chinese government must shut down those small coal mines that do not have the conditions for safe production, that does not comply with industrial policies, waste resources, and that pollute the environment. If they want to continue the production, they must incorporate the completion of the target of eliminating backward production capacity into the performance appraisal system of local governments, and consequently to make the target completion of reducing backward production capacity meet with the performance appraisal system made by the local government. To strictly implement the "Coking Industry Access Conditions (2008 revision) and the relevant environmental protection policies, to implement the principle of sustainable development of "total control, adjustment of structure, conservation of energy and resources, protection of the environment and rational distribution," to complete the country's elimination of the backward production capacity of the coke industry's goal (Bai and Zhang, 2017).

In addition, the Chinese government must strengthen the export management of environmental products. To further expand the opening to the outside and accumulate construction funds. Continue to expand exports. It is the strategic policy of China. At the same time, for the shipping of some products with distinct environmental factors, management must be strengthened. In limiting the export of coke, the state has repeatedly raised the coke export tariffs. In May 2004, after China abolished the export tax rebate on coke, the export tariffs were repeatedly raised, from 5% in November 2006 to 15% in June 2007, to 25% in January 2008 and 40% in August, and have been maintained since then. Practice shows that the tariff adjustment has curbed the blind investment in some places and stopped the short-sightedness for exportation of the ecological environment of hometown for profit-making. Of course, the use of economic instruments should be moderate, beneficial with restraint, and avoid possible incidents such as WTO complaints, arbitration, and so on. Some overseas businessmen are greedy, taking one's undeserved gain for granted, so China cannot let them do that (Li, 2017).

On January 29, 2007, the Ministry of Finance and State Administration of Taxation issued on the adjustment of coking coal resource tax standards for tax notice (No.15 document of Finance and Taxation, 2007) to adjust the coking coal resource tax, determining the applicable tax standard of the resource tax of coking coal which is mainly used for cooking, as 8 yuan per ton. Coking coal is listed as the first adjustment of the new resource tax, showing the scarcity of the resource in the market. In 2010, the state began the pilot project of resource tax reform in Xinjiang Uygur Autonomous Region. It collected a 5% resource tax on crude oil and natural gas, according to the ad valorem levy (Liu and Liu, 2017).

Although such reforms have not involved coal at present, the implementation of this reform is an inevitable trend, which is conducive to the formation of a pattern of total costs and paid use of resources. However, the resource tax as an essential means of adjustment of coal differential rent, the current method of collecting tax and low taxes is not conducive to improving the efficiency of resource extraction. To curb the rapid growth of coal consumption and make the coke industry better able to develop through price leverage, China needs to promote coke futures actively. In this way, the exchange can try to focus on high-end coke products when making coke contracts, which will help to protect China's high-end technology and resources of coke.

The EU RoHS directive, which has entered into force on July 1, 2006, restricts the amount of 4 kinds of heavy metals in electronic and electrical products. The standard is stringent. The maximum limits specified in the directive are as follows: Pb < 1000mg/Kg; Hg < 1000mg/Kg; Cd < 100mg/Kg; Cr6+ < 1000mg/Kg etc. Independent assessment shows that the human body is exposed to these four heavy metals, and the health will be damaged. For example, lead can cause the central nervous system to be affected. Cadmium causes injury to bones, kidneys, and respiratory system. Mercury affects the central nervous system and kidney system, and six valence chromium causes genetic defects. Countries such as the United Kingdom, the United States, the European Union, and other countries and international organizations have a long history of identifying and managing PBT chemical substances and have accumulated some experience and formed certain systems (Wang, Yang, and Yan, 2011). China can learn from and innovate advanced methods and adopt independent assessment methods to evaluate the PBT chemical substances of domestic important and needed. Based on the evaluation results, China will formulate rules that are not only in line with international standards but also promote the development of domestic green products. This will effectively promote the domestic production of high-quality mechanical and electrical products and also help to solve the green barriers (Wang and Tian, 2012).

In the case of strengthening the forest carbon exchange transaction, there are two critical measures to develop a low carbon economy, save energy, reduce emission, and beautify the environment. The first is industrial emission reduction, called direct emission reduction; the second is forest carbon sequestration, which is called indirect emission reduction. According to the Seventh National Forest Resources Inventory (2004 - 2008), artificial afforestation of Chinese preservation area reached 62 million hectares, ranking first in the world; the national forest area reached 195 million hectares; the forest coverage rate increased from 13.92% to 20.36% in the early 1990s, two years earlier completed, two years ahead of the 2010 forest coverage (Wang and Mao, 2011).

According to the results of this survey and the monitoring results of forest ecological location, the total carbon reserves of forest vegetation in China reached 7811 million tons. The forest green system of water conservation volume reached 494 billion 766 million cubic meters, annual soil volume reached 7035 million tons, the annual amount of fertilizer reached 364 million tons, and the yearly absorption of atmospheric pollutant volume reached 32 million tons, annual dust volume reached 5001 million tons. Only six functions of ecosystem services, such as carbon fixation, oxygen release, water conservation, conservation of soil, purification of atmospheric environment, accumulation of nutrients, and biodiversity protection, can create wealth, with an annual value of 10 trillion and 10 billion Yuan. Increasing afforestation efforts and developing forest carbon trading have far-reaching significance.

Therefore, China must continue to implement and fulfill the "Outline for the Twelfth Five-year Plan for National Economic and Social Development" reviewed and approved by the Fourth Session of the 11th National People's Congress (NPC) in March 2011. The law includes the forest coverage, forest volume of two forest indicators as a binding indicator into the national economic and social development planning. At the same time, the State Forestry Administration made specific arrangements for the examination of two restrictive signs in 2012. They have become an essential part of the comprehensive assessment of local governments at the national level. Planting trees is to protect the environment and benefit the children and grandchildren (Zhang, 2017).

The most appropriate way to reduce greenhouse gas emissions on a global scale is to participate in the UN-led international climate negotiations and actions. China has been participating in international climate negotiations and has played a decisive role. In June 2007, the Chinese government first set forth a "National Plan to Address Climate Change" in developing countries. In those days, China actively and constructively participated in the UN climate change talks in Bali, Indonesia, making a substantive contribution to the formation of the Bali road map. At that conference, China made three recommendations. For example, adherence to the provision of financial resources and technology transfer to developing countries is well implemented. These were endorsed by all the participants and eventually incorporated into the road map (He and Chen, 2012).

In 2009, China actively participated in the Copenhagen conference negotiations; announced the Implementation of the Bali Road Map - the Chinese Government's Position on the Copenhagen Climate Change Conference, put forward China's principles and goals for the Copenhagen conference. It plays a crucial role in breaking the deadlock of the negotiations and promoting the consensus of the parties. In 2010, China fully participated in the talks and consultations at the Cancun Conference in Mexico, insisted on maintaining openness, extensive participation, and consensus in the negotiation process. Before the Cancun Conference in the United Nations, China hosted a UN climate change conference in Tianjin province, laying the foundation for a positive outcome at Cancun.

China actively participates in related international scientific and technological cooperation programs under the framework of the Earth Science System Alliance, such as the World Climate Research Program, the National Geosphere-Biosphere Program, the National Human Dimensions Plan for Global Change, the Global Earth Observation System of Inter-governmental Coordination, the Global Climate System Observations Project, the relevant research results provide a useful reference for the formulation of China's climate change policy. China has established a mechanism for dialogue and cooperation in the field of climate change with the United States, the European Union, Italy, Germany, Norway, the United Kingdom, France, Australia, Canada, Japan, and other countries and regions, signed relevant joint statements, memorandums of understanding and cooperation agreements, linking climate change as an essential part of the cooperation between the two parties (Geng, 2017).

China will continue to adhere to the two-track negotiation mechanism of the "UN Framework Convention on Climate Change" and the "Kyoto Protocol" in the future, insisting the rules of the parties dominated, open and transparent, extensive participation and consensus. China must give full play to the main channel of international negotiations on climate change within the framework of the U.N. and adhere to the principle of common but differentiated responsibilities. China will actively and constructively participate in the talks, strengthen communication and exchanges with all parties, promote consensus among all parties, and achieve results for the U.N. climate negotiations (Li, 2017).

The earth is the only homeland of humankind in the universe. Protecting the earth's environment is the condition for preserving the survival and development of humanity.

Conclusion

Innovation is the source of momentum for social progress. Change is also full of twists and turns. It is a fact that China's environmental pollution is severe, which could generate a negative impact on the progress of the "One Belt One Road" construction. To solve this dilemma is to rely on innovative guidelines. The level of China's industrialization development currently belongs to the second half of the mid-industrialization period. Environmental problems are particularly prominent. Some mass-caused environmental incidents have caused severe problems. Therefore, it is of considerable significance to apply the game theory and so on to analyze the real issues in depth. Thinking from the perspective of competition in the international market, looking for ways to solve these problems, and making an analysis of the future direction are the core concepts of this chapter (Wang and Tian, 2012).

There are more than 60 countries along with one belt one road, all are with different national conditions and different cultural backgrounds, and China must seek and rely on the greatest common divisor in achieving equality and mutual benefit and realizing inclusive development under the principle of common difference. The environment protection undertaking is full of tensions in the transition and the game of interests. China's environmental situation is at a crossroads during the implementation of the Five-year Plans. Therefore, China must deal with the different objective requirements of the government, residents, and enterprises or balance the different tendencies of interests. In the process of China's development, the coke production, the zigzag export trade, and the technical barriers of other products all have the distinctive typical significance. China must correctly understand the three E.U. directives with environmental protection factors to deal with the harsh international challenges honestly. China has made a lot of contributions to actively participating in the climate negotiations under the U.N. framework. There is a bright future for China's environmental protection and economical construction, along with the progress of the "One Belt One Road" construction.

Chapter 6
A Super Strong vs. A Group Strong

"One Belt One Road" is a new attempt to achieve economic globalization initiated by China's leadership. The economic and social development of the participating countries is still very uneven, and demands are different. In the globalization and multi-polarization, the development of the world is still unpredictable as there are still many uncertainties in the world economic development. Realizing the vision of "One Belt One Road" is not only a matter of advocacy but also the participation of all participants. Only with the joint efforts of all parties, can the related countries jointly meet the challenges, seek common development and create a new world of sustained prosperity on the new platform of the community of common destiny for humankind. Under this premise, it is undoubtedly of great significance to explore the future world political and economic pattern, whether it is unipolar development or multi-polarization development, and whether a super strong power exists alone or a group of strong countries exists at the same time.

Introduction

It cannot be decided by China's national strength solely whether China can become a world leader and whether she can become a competent leader. China must consider the international situation she is facing as well. So, what is the current global situation? In this regard, China should examine from many areas (Huan, 1989). As China develops and expands gradually, all countries begin to discuss the latest evolution of the world situation. Is it a super strong or a group of strong? Or return to the bipolar era? Is it another "battlefield" for experts and scholars to express their opinions? What role will China play in the development and changes of the world pattern? Is it true that China will act as the world police and share the entire world with the United States? Maybe history will give us the answer (Feng, 1988).

Since the end of World War II, the two significant camps of capitalism and socialism led by the United States and the former Soviet Union have ceased to exist after a series of major international events such as the Cold War, the drastic changes in Eastern Europe and the Soviet Union (Li, 1989). The world entered the era of a so-called super strong, which is referring to the United States. And the ending of the bipolar pattern started with the 1991 landmark events (Feng and Song, 1992). On the night of December 25, 1991, the Soviet Union flag decorated with sickle axes and the red five-pointed star was pulled down on the Red Square in Moscow under the watchful eyes of the world, which is the most distressing thing for the former Soviet Union leaders and the socialist countries. It announced that the Soviet Union was over as well as the end of the history of Marxism-Leninism. There had been 69 years for the Soviet Socialist Union. Finally, it came to the end of history, and the Soviet Union as a country is no longer existing today legally (Zhang, 2001).

The world situation turned from the U.S.-Soviet hegemony to one super strong power in the world from then on. Chinese President Hu Jintao made the following statement: The world today is undergoing significant changes and adjustments. Peace and development are still the topics of the times. Seeking peace, seeking growth, and promoting cooperation have become an irresistible trend of the times. The international situation is generally stable, but there are still some unsettled factors. Hegemonism and power politics still exist. Local conflicts come one after another, and world peace and development are facing many challenges (Hu, 2007). This statement made by Hu Jintao reflects the Chinese leaders' judgments entirely on the current international situation.

The principle of Marxist philosophy emphasizes that the development and movement are absolute for anything, while stillness is relative. The development and evolution of the international situation are under constant changes. In the last century, the global political and economic patterns remained West dominated, headed by the United States. The United States was a super strong power, and several strong capabilities coexisted at the same time. As the only superpower in the world, the United States was in the center of global power, and Europe, Japan, China, and Russia were behind her (Ros, Delgado and Vila, 2003). As a result, one side was the United States. The other team was composed of Europe, Japan, China, and Russia. These two sides' comparison became the new pattern of international relations. This is what we call the world pattern in which there was a super strong power together with multiple capabilities (Liu, 2018).

After years, the position of the United States as the overlord of the world has been seriously threatened by the deepening of economic globalization and the rise of other countries in the world (Li, 2015). Under a series of financial crises and the pressures from the rise of big powers, it has become a hot topic widely discussed by people whether the United States can maintain her hegemony position above all and stabilize the other powerful countries. Some people think that the world today is still the unipolar era in which the United States dominates (Huang, 2003). They admit that the United States is a super-strong power while denying the decline of the United States; they believe that the era of one superpower coexisting with multiple controls has not come to an end. Some other people think that this kind of situation has ended, and there forms a group of powers that are rising rapidly. With the enhancement of China's economic strength and the continuous improvement of her overall national strength (Xu, 2001), and the gradual deepening of the EU integration, the United States is no longer a world leader anymore. There will occur a group of strong powers, which can be called multipolar, but not unipolar any more. The world's hegemony is the strength of all countries, but not one of them, which is recognized and supported by the Chinese people, from the understanding of Chinese people.

Background for a Super Strong and a Group Strong

The disintegration of the Soviet Union, the end of the Cold War, the disintegration of the bipolar structure, and the United States becoming the sole superpower, all these brought many changes in many aspects. On the one hand, the desire of the U.S. government to dominate the world has been inflated further. Therefore, the hegemonist and unilateralist foreign policies have been stepped up. On the other hand, the old balance has been broken, and the new balance can hardly be established for a while. Significant changes have taken place in the inter-relations between the muscular powers, including the hostile countries during the Cold War. Many countries, including the allies of the United States, required that the United States should promote joint development and prosperity through dialogue and cooperation with mutual respect, equality and mutual benefit, thus making it more and more difficult for the United States to push for the unilateral expansion (Guo and Li, 2018).

Since the Cold War ended, the speed and scale of the European reunification and independence and self-improvement have drawn the world's attention. The EU implemented the Maastricht Treaty, expanded and improved the stock market, issued the euro, established a currency union, and promoted the universal foreign policies and defense plans, then pushed the unified constitutional reform as well as enlarging the European Union and NATO so that Europe would become an essential member of the pluralistic world effectively. They made their voices, put forward their ideas, built an image of an overall strength (Ji, 2017).

Let us look at China's action. Since China implemented the reform and opening, she has been advancing along the road of socialism with Chinese characteristics and has enjoyed rapid economic growth. Her achievements in construction have attracted worldwide attention. Her comprehensive national strength has been enhanced significantly, her politics and society have maintained long-term stability, and China's international status has been dramatically improved (Zhen, 2017). Although China's national strength still lags far behind that of the developed countries in the West, as the largest developing country in the world, China's peaceful rise and the adherence to her principle and the non-alignment spirit in the international community have made a significant impact on the world pattern (Wang, 2018).

All these facts show that it is irresistible for the world situation to become multi-polarized. The multi-polarization means that there are many "power centers," which are interdependent, cooperative, competitive, mutually influential, and mutually constraining. Regarding this kind of trend and the pattern that it forms, we may summarize as "one super strong." It must be known that the number of countries which admit multi-polarity and advocate the establishment of a multipolar world is increasing. This phenomenon is undoubtedly a portrayal of the times in which all the strong powers have risen together. It is an inevitable phenomenon to turn from one pole to an era of multi-polarization gradually. Under such a global pattern, people's necessary consensus is that this constructive process of multipolarity in international relations helps to establish a new order of balance, stability, democracy, and non-confrontation, which is in the fundamental interest of all countries (Yu, 2005).

On-surface development and progress do not indicate that everything satisfies people (Yu, 2000). The consensus meeting the fundamental interests of most countries objectively does not belong to the United States. After the world comes to the era of "one super strong," the "one super strong" here means the United States, and she has tried her best to promote the "unipolar world" under her leadership and to discourage the process of multi-polarization. Although the United States has made various efforts for this purpose, it has occupied a high place as the world leader and acted as the world police. However, the world pattern of multi-polarization in the political economy has become a trend of the times, and the United States cannot block it. Of course, from time to time, there will still be arguments about denying the multi-polarization of the world (Jin and Zhang, 2018).

Some people still think that the world pattern is always the unipolar pattern headed by the United States (Wang and Li, 1987). The United States will not be able to sway her position as a world leader in world domination. The main reason for this argument may be due to these two considerations: Firstly, to confuse the fact that the United States is the sole superpower in the current world with the unipolar world; secondly, to compare the world's multi-polarization with the multi-polar world the multipolar world has not been formed yet, but we cannot deny the multi-polarization which already exists undoubtedly. Is it a super strong or a group of strong on earth? If you want to have a clear understanding with regards to the current world situation, you had better rationalize the relations among the influential powers in the world (Qiu, 2017).

Evolving to "A Group Strong"

The "a super-strong" international relations have been formed since the early 1990s and has undergone more than a decade of development and evolution (Tina and Dai, 2014), it created an apparent multi-polarization pattern which we can see today. During this period, the following two features have been showing:

Number one, the single-polarization, and multi-polarization have been coexisting and will continue to fight (Chen, 1985). As an integrated international relations pattern, the pattern of "one super strong" tends to become: single-super-polarization plus a multi-strong-polarization. On the one hand, as the sole superpower, the United States promotes unilateralism actively and attempts to establish the unipolar world headed by the United States. On the other hand, under the impetus of economic globalization, the China's rise, the European integration, Japan's seeking political and military power, and the slow recovery of the Russian economy, all these show that the multi-polarization is about to come, and pose a considerable challenge to the unipolarity pursued by the United States. Therefore, the result is that the United States will not be able to dominate the entire world, and the trend of multi-polarization in the world will continue. The coexistence of single-polarization and multi-polarization will keep unchanged for a long time (Xu, 2018).

Number two is the formation of unipolar pluralism. The multipolar world pattern today inherits the duality from the old bipolar model

(Shen and Zhao, 2005). In the bipolar structure, the two sides opposing the international strategic forces are the United States and the Soviet Union. However, the dualistic confrontation in today's multi-dimensional world has become the "one super" United States and the "multi-strong" - the EU, China and Russia, India, and many other world powers. It has become a diversified world landscape. Although under the condition of economic globalization, the confrontation between "one super and multi-strong" is not as intense as the Cold War between the United States and the Soviet Union. However, the relationship between the multi-strong and the relationship between "one super" and "multi-strong" are becoming more and more complicated. The scope and situation of competitors are also becoming more extensive and complicated. After entering the twenty-first century, the pattern of "A super-strong" after the Cold War was changed gradually. This was shown in the following three aspects:

Firstly, the emerging market economy was occurring. With the historic opportunity of globalization, some emerging market economy countries such as China, India, Russia, and Brazil pushed forward their internal reforms and made fantastic achievements. Their international status and influence were also increasing. All these achievements were impacting the United States' world leader position. The results produced by these mentioned countries led to the decline of the dominance by the western world headed by the United States. The most obvious manifestation of this is the evolution of the G8 meeting to the "G20" meeting (Rhee, 2011). This shows that many global political, economic, trade, and environmental issues will no longer be solved in the G8 system. Therefore, these emerging economies must be invited to participate in the decision-making process. This phenomenon shows that it is now over for the developed countries to dominate the international system and international issues (Kim and Chung, 2012).

Secondly, the contradictions between the western countries headed by the United States and Russia have been increased (Trabelsi, 2011). The geopolitical confrontation between the United States and Russia and the security contradiction between these two countries have existed for a long time. A lot of them are the continuation of the disagreements between the United States and the Soviet Union during the Cold War. The conflicts between the United States and the Islamic world are due to the differences in culture, beliefs, and values between them. The new trend now is that Russia can combine with Islamic extremists to fight against the United States. If this combination occurs, it will inevitably lead to further contradictions between the United States and the outside world, and the international environment will be even worse (Daugherty and Pfalzgraf, 2003).

Thirdly, some slight changes have taken place in the internal relations of the western allies led by the United States, showing the trend of reverse evolution. The world-leading position for the United States is benefited from these two: muscular national strength and stable alliance system. Europe is an essential part of the U.S. alliance system, and NATO is the most important mechanism. After the Cold War, due to the disintegration of the external joint opponent-the Soviet Union, Europe's desire to cooperate with the U.S. has been declining (Nye, 1992), and the differences in the significant threat perceptions have been growing. Especially after the Iraq war, the conflicts between the United States and what Bush called "Old Europe" was even more acute. Besides, with the progress of European integration, the EU has become the leading force in European politics, economy, diplomacy, and security and has gained more independence from the United States (Nasser, etc., 2015).

The EU is facing a crisis caused by the debt crisis. Therefore, the European countries will mainly focus on resolving and strengthening EU internal solidarity in their affairs and will not be able to bear too much responsibility for NATO, which is contrary to the United States. Besides, the economic and trade conflicts between the United States and Europe have increased. The rise of the euro has hit the cornerstone of U.S. hegemony-the dollar hegemony and has an impact on U.S. interests. Although those countries that use euro as their currency are facing a severe debt crisis, the euro as the world currency still has a more significant deterrent to the dollar's hegemony (Xue, 2018).

The World Pattern in Current Times

From the above, we can see that the relations between big powers are an essential reflection of how the world situation has formed; the changes in the relationships among big powers today reflect the formation of the world's political and economic pattern. The characteristics of world powers relations are as follows: Firstly, peace and development are still the main topics for our current times. All countries in the world, whether it is a vast country or a small one, almost all of them regard economic development as the primary goal, and they enhance their comprehensive competitiveness through various methods. Evolution is the absolute principle. Therefore, all countries follow the policy of peaceful coexistence and mutual benefit for joint development and seek development through competition. Secondly, the relations among big powers have paramount strategic significance, considering its long-term, comprehensive and complex relationships. "Strategic relations" and "partnership" without the alliance are the new things during the multi-polarization after the Cold War and become a unique transitional phenomenon in the reconstruction of a new international economic and political order. Thirdly, the economic factor is the primary and decisive factor in the relations among major powers. The premise for the adjustment of the relationships between major powers is to seek, coordinate, and balance each other's economic interests. Diplomacy based on economic integration and economic complementarity will benefit both parties. Fourthly, the democratization of international politics will become an essential goal in the adjustment of the relations among big powers. Opposing cold war mentality, hegemonism, and power politics will be an unavoidable long-term task in the alignment of the relationships between major powers (Yu, 2005).

What is the reason for the formation of the world multi-polarization trend? The pattern of "one super strong" international relations is not a static structure, but a dynamic one with the unipolar and multipolar contradictions. Multipolarization is the primary trend. Looking at the political and economic situations in the world today, maintaining peace and promoting development have become irreversible trends. The relations among big powers are becoming diversified gradually. Since the American President Obama took over the United States from Bush, the United States has brought the world a global economic crisis. It has brought a furious war to Iraqi and Afghan people and a substantial fiscal deficit for the country. Besides, the European debt crisis affected the economy and politics of Europe in varying degrees. In this context, a subtle change happened to the relations among the world powers, the political and economic situation in the world has shifted to multipole gradually. The era of multi-polarization with "a group of strong" is now coming (Wang, 2018).

It is well known that things will develop in the opposite direction when they become extreme, and in the case of the United States, it is going to be declined after being prosperous too much. Neo-realism thinks that the promotion of unilateral hegemony and control of the international system can gain economic benefits, but it also must pay a corresponding price. In the hegemony system, the dominant state will expand until it reaches a balance between the costs and benefits. Once it reaches that equilibrium, the value for maintaining the international status will be higher than that for its economic growth (Gilpin, 2007). When economic power is difficult to sustain the expansion costs, the dominant state is forced to halt its expansion The unipolar structure is the apex of the development of the hegemonic state when reaching this apex, it will not be possible for the United States to grow her resources again, and she will reduce the cost of maintaining expansion and weaken its hegemony After the Cold War ended, the leadership of the United States reached her apex. She launched the Kosovo war, the war in Afghanistan, the war in Iraq. During the administration of George W. Bush, the arrogance of her unilateralism and the hegemony policy reached the limit in the world. However, these hegemonism activities also consume the strength of the United States. Unilateralism's unfavorable factors will lead the United States to decline. Wars will only accelerate this process but will not help the United States' hegemony (Su, 2018).

Under the conditions of economic globalization, the comparative advantage of the United States in the economic field has been decreasing, and the economic forces have begun to spread globally. Since the 1970s, there occurred three transfers in the world's economic effects. That is, the advantages of economic power have shifted from the United States to other major powers, from developed countries to developing countries and from western countries to non-western countries. The first transfer led to the tripartite confrontation of the U.S., Japan, and Europe in the capitalist world. The second transfer has enhanced the economic position for the developing countries. It is clear that this transfer has generated a challenge to the United States. At the same time, international organizations formed by developing countries, such as the Non-Aligned Movement, the Organization of Petroleum Exporting Countries, and the ASEAN, are consolidating the power of the developing countries and promoting their development while improving the multi-polarization of the international economic structure. The third transfer has allowed many non-Western countries to gain rapid economic growth and let the U.S. economy be decreased (Xiao, 2015).

After entering the 21st century, the emerging economic countries, for example, the "Diamond 11 Countries" (Bangladesh, Egypt, Indonesia, Mexico, Nigeria, Pakistan, the Philippines, the United Republic of Korea, Turkey, Vietnam), they accelerated the multi-polarization trend of the international economic structure. The emerging countries have formed their economic development model per their national conditions. It also broke the single American development model promoted by the "Washington consensus," and the diversification of the development model has become an essential part of the multiploidization (Wang and Wei, 2009).

In the international political area, most of countries oppose the unipolar world. China advocates multilateralism in settlement of foreign affairs. France claims that his view on a multi-polar world is intensifying. Russia believes that the multi-polar world is "the most sensible and democratic international social system." Also, many global issues such as environmental problems, non-traditional security, and the global financial crisis that emerged during world development cannot be settled by a few considerable powers or even by one or two superpowers. At the same time, it may be solved after promoting multilateralism. For example, to cope with the current global financial crisis triggered by the United States, the international dialogue mechanism was upgraded from G8 to the G20, this kind of upgrade was a manifestation of the multilateralism development. "Multi-polarization and multilateralism are complementary and mutually reinforcing: the precondition of multi-polarization is that multiple strength centers are based on equal terms, which is in line with the basic principle of multilateralism. Regarding the modern multilateralism, which is emerged to cope with the financial crisis, it brought opportunities for multi-polarization development." (Liu, 2009)

In addition, the U.S. military strength seems to be too powerless to maintain a unipolar world. The United States owns the most powerful military force in the world. However, the major powers in the world will not obey him if only relying on his advantage of military strength. It cannot make up for the shortcoming in other fields. As a "trump card" for the United States to promote unipolarity, the role of durable military power in influencing international relations has been significantly reduced. The Iraqi war and the war in Afghanistan have highlighted the inadequacies of the U.S. military. The technological superiority of the United States has also been challenged. Robert Gilpin, a famous scholar of international relations and international politics, believes that the transfer of advanced technology from an advanced society to a backward society is undoubtedly an essential reason for the power redistribution in the global system. The United States has world-class sciences and technologies that support economic development. To maintain his technological superiority, the United States adopted an export control policy to limit the proliferation of technology-intensive industries (Fang and Sun, 2014).

However, under the condition of economic globalization, the technologies were already increased because of the international cooperation and international labor division. Some countries will form a "backward advantage" after adopting advanced technologies, which is a challenge to the United States' technological superiority. The revival of non-Western civilization has challenged the hegemony of the Western culture headed by the United States. After the 1970s, the improvement of non-Western civilizations, such as Confucianism civilization, Japanese civilization, Indian civilization, Orthodox civilization, Indian civilization, and Islamic civilization, shows the diversification of world soft power and will break the domination of Western civilization finally. As Huntington once indicated: Power is shifting from Western culture to non-Western civilization, and global politics have become multipolar and multi-civilized (Liu, 2009).

From the above reasons, it is not difficult to realize that it is a requirement of times for the world economic pattern to evolve toward multi-polarization, it is in the interest of people in all countries, and it is an inevitable outcome under the background of economic globalization. Economic globalization has enabled all kinds of production factors to be optimized and configured globally, promoted the rapid development of the global economy, and even encouraged the formation of a multipolar world. The multipolar pattern has led all forces in the world to form a relationship of mutual developing and mutual restraint, to avoid the outbreak of a new world war, and to a certain extent, curb the further development of hegemonism and power politics, and promote the establishment of a fair and reasonable new international political and economic order, and finally, will bring a new world of peace, stability, and prosperity, for all people in the world. Also, it will help the developing countries grasp the opportunity to develop themselves, especially for China, who want to seek further development in the complex international relations (Luo, 2014).

At the same time, we should also know that it will be a long, tortuous, and complicated process for the evolution of multi-polarization. In this process, the conflicts between unipolar and multi-polar, the struggles between hegemony and non-hegemony, will last for a long time. Competitions contain cooperation, and cooperation also includes race, this is an essential feature during the multi-polarization development. In the struggles between the world's multi-polarization and unilateralism, military power is significant. For the excellent skills in the world, almost all of them attempted to establish a strong national defense force. They tried to strengthen their military's role in safeguarding and expanding the national interest to occupy a dominant position in the world multi-polarization, for the strategic initiative in the 21st-century international community. In the increasingly fierce competition for comprehensive national strength, the status of the economy and technology is becoming more and more critical. The muscular economic and technological power is the fundamental condition for becoming a world leader. Therefore, all countries give priority to economic development. It depends on the rapid economic development of the world's major powers and the developing countries, whether the world multi-polarization can become a reality (Sun, 2012).

Peace and Development are Current Themes

For the past and the present, is the world pattern "a super-strong" or "a group of strong?" What is the specific status of this pattern? For the past, the answer is clear; for the present, the scholars seem to have no clear and definite answer. Most scholars agree with this opinion: the bipolar structure has been dissolved, and various forces redistributed. The world has been moving toward multi-polarization. The formation of a new pattern will take a long time. From the historical experience, some scholars described that the unipolar model is volatile. From the reality of international politics, they emphasized the transitional and complex nature of the current global situation as well as the uncertainty in the adjustment of foreign forces. At the same time, they think that the United States' unipolar opinion remains stubborn. However, this statement has some problems, because it only emphasizes the current transition period between the old pattern and the new one, but does not conduct any further analysis of the pattern of the transitional period. Therefore, the remaining question is, how should we accurately conclude the current world pattern? After the war in Kosovo, there have also been some different voices in academia. Some scholars think that the world today is where the unipolar forces of the United States rule the world. Multi-polarization is only our wishful thinking. These different understandings result from the qualitative ambiguity of the general pattern. To improve, it requires the follow-up efforts of our relevant scholars (He, 2011).

The world situation was formed under the control of various forces. There is no such thing as a "vacuum" in the balance of forces, or a "blank" situation in the general pattern. In any period of history or reality, there always existed some contrasts for various effects. It is impossible to have no orientation or no pattern. In other words, if somebody says there is no world pattern at all, he must be lying. Watching from the global international situation, there would be three types of world patterns: unipolar, bipolar, and multipolar. If we refer to these three typical patterns as "safflower," we will inevitably ask what the "green leaves" are? There must still be many patterns that acted as "transition" between these two, which can be called "green leaves" accordingly. Based on this analysis, it is reasonable to think that the parallel structure of international forces after the Cold War is referring to the United States as the only super strong country and several other "strong countries," that is, the unipolar and multivariate world structure. Unipolarity is the only world power that refers specifically to "the United States." In contrast, diversity refers to many regional authorities or regional groups such as the EU, Russia, Japan, and China. This unipolar multivariate pattern has both the tendency of unipolarity and the tendency of multi-polarization (Gelpern, 2011).

Undoubtedly, the United States occupied a dominant position in the post-Cold-War international pattern, and thus she became "a super-strong." At the same time, the multi-polarization of the global pattern after the cold war was also developing. For the European Union, which played a significant role in the multipolar world, her strategic goal is to restore and establish the status of the former "world center" in Europe and to continue to speed up the European integration. Russia is also adjusting her foreign policy constantly to restore her status as a former superpower. Although Japan always hides under the umbrella of the United States, she does not forget her mission; her goal of moving toward a political power remains unchanged. She has been increasing her international obligations and responsibilities gradually in foreign affairs, participating in several global peacekeeping operations, and she has attempted to become a permanent member of the UN Security Council. China has become active in the international arena increasingly and has maintained its stable growth. Also, China has become a necessary positive force in the readjustment of significant powers and has promoted the multi-polarization of the world effectively. And China has always stood for peace and development, which is an essential topic of current times (Semmler and Young, 2010).

Why peace and development are still the topics of our current times? In addition to the things that the Chinese People have learned in their political textbooks, the Chinese People can regard themselves as out-of-school scholars or bystanders. The overall situation is that the world needs peace, and people call for peace. All those things that were done by hegemonism and power politics are all strongly opposed by people in all countries in the world. Please do not say that those protests are useless, nor should they assume that opposition is just a bluff. You must know that people like water and the water can carry boats, and the boats can be capsized by the water as well. Once the people were infuriated, what are the rulers in the eyes of the public? The governments of various countries also dare not ignore this issue, even in the United States, they convince their people with the idea of the "American dream" regularly. For what? That is to calm the public anger, calm the people, tell people that the present is temporary, and the future will be bright (Li and Huang, 2017).

The peaceful development of the world is the common aspiration of all peoples, and it is an irresistible historical trend. "People will survive if obeying the trend, or he will die." This is the truth. Local and small-scale turmoil can only be regarded as the small conflicts next to this mainstream, and it requires the noble spirit of stepping on the coast for peaceful development.

The Outlook for World Future

The current multi-polar world is still changing from time to time. The final formation of a multi-polar structure will take a long time. In this process, many unfavorable factors may block the creation and development of a multi-level structure. What will the world pattern be in the future? When will it be formed finally? This depends on the gambling stratagem among the major powers in the current world. The unsafe and unstable factors in the current international situation are also significant aspects of disrupting the world structure. These insecurity and instability are mainly manifested in the following areas:

Firstly, the conflicts among the major powers still exist. In 2011, there happened some complicated changes in the international situation. The financial crisis was deepened, the wars happened in some areas, and the Asia-Pacific strategic importance was rising. Despite the marked improvement in the relations among big powers in recent years, the friction and conflicts of interests were also increasing. There existed some contradictions between the rise of unilateralism and the strengthening of multilateral cooperation in the international community. In the near future, the development of the relations among the major powers will be further tested by the Middle East issue, the North Korean nuclear issue, and so on. The relationships between China and the United States will also continue to be tested by the Taiwan issue, the Diaoyu Islands issue, the South China Sea and other territorial issues (Wang and Zhou, 2017).

Secondly, the prospects for world economic development are not optimistic. At present, the world economy has not been out of the doldrums fully and is still facing severe uncertainties. In 2011, those who were already out of the doldrums was stilling in the recovering process. Those institutions that had made optimistic forecasts earlier have downgraded their forecasts for world economic growth recently. In September 2011, the International Monetary Fund estimated that the global output in 2011 would reach 78.85 trillion U.S. dollars by purchasing power parity (PPP), an increase of 4.47 trillion U.S. dollars from the previous year, with a real growth rate of 4.0%, down 0.4 percent from its forecast in April 2011; GDP at market exchange rates will exceed 70.01 trillion U.S. dollars, up to the U.S. $ 7.10 trillion from the previous year, but the real growth rate will be revised downwards from 3.5% to 3.0%, down 0.5 percent. In December 2010, Goldman Sachs predicted that the world economy would grow by 4.6% in 2011, while in the August 2011 report, Goldman Sachs lowered the figure by 0.5 percentage point to 4.0%. The overall trend of world economic development since 2011 is a downward trend. It has dropped to 2.2% in 2016 and lost by nearly 1.8 percentage points from 2011. The United Nations estimated that the global economic growth in 2017 would increase from 2.2% to 2.7%, and in 2018 it will be 2.9%. The outlook for global economic development is still not optimistic (Chen, 2017).

This situation is not due to the lack of resources and capacity to solve problems in the world today, but because of the fragmentation and exclusiveness of international cooperation. It is difficult to integrate resources effectively, especially in the recent stage, due to the impact of COVID-19, the trend of "anti-globalization" has risen, and the contradictions between openness and conservatism, reform and conservatism, economic integration and "fragmentation" have become increasingly prominent. The continuous occurrence of the "black swan" incident has brought great uncertainty to the world development and also brought variables to the deep international economic and trade cooperation. In response to this new trend of international political and economic development, China should be able to take on the responsibility of a big country, continue to hold the banner of economic globalization and free trade, actively seek solutions to the problems facing the world and regional economy, stimulate new momentum of world economic growth with the steady and sustainable growth of China's economy, and promote the construction and improvement of a new order of global economic governance. China should work closely with the international community to inject new energy into the realization of linkage development.

Thirdly, the emotional issues in some areas are severe. These issues include the Iranian nuclear issue, the North Korea nuclear issue, the North Korean crisis, the internal political contradictions in the former socialist countries in Eastern Europe and the Near East, the Taiwan issue, the issue of the Diaoyu Islands, the effect of the South China Sea and so on.

So, what will the pattern be in the future world? Governed or chaos? We need to seek truth from facts. China must make a reasonable presumption of the future pattern in the world according to the current multi-polarization trend, the power balance among the world powers, and the reasonable prediction of the future world. Regarding the pattern of the future world, different countries have different opinions. Taking this two countries-China and the United States as an example, in March 2012, the United States published a cover article in its "Times," predicting the ten significant trends affecting the world in the next ten years, emphasizing that the 21st century is a United States century, it extended the G2 concept to "axis" for the first time. China is reluctant to accept the U.S. statement. The United States has drawn China into the axis. Of course, China will not admit the self-centered arrogance of the United States. There are still some people who think that China will rise gradually, Europe will become more unified, the wars will continue, the United States, Russia, China and Europe, these four are going to be the most significant four parties in the world (Lane, 2010).

After all, how the world's political and economic pattern evolves depends on the political and financial strength of various countries. Therefore, how the future world structure develops depends on the political and economic power of all countries in the world today. According to the current financial strength of major powers, the power balance among big powers will ultimately result in a relatively stable multipolar world structure. Whether the multi-polar world structure will finally come into existence or not and how long it will take to form will depend on the strength of the countries in the world in terms of politics, economy, military affairs and so forth. Therefore, all countries should pay attention to developing their economic strength, adopt the Marxist theories; the financial foundation determines the superstructure. No matter how the world economic structure changes, China should deal with the ever-changing forms of the world with an unchanged development concept (Tian and Dai, 2014).

Conclusion

"A super-strong" and "a group of strong" will eventually form a stable pattern of multi-polarization in the world. This outcome is in line with the "One Belt One Road" initiatives proposed by the Chinese leadership. Peace and development are still the topics of current times in the world, which is the immediate international background for China to promote the "One Belt One Road" construction. However, peace and development are facing challenges that cannot be ignored. The unjust and unreasonable international political and economic old order has not changed yet. As a result, some local and small-scale wars, tension and turmoil still exist, the North-South gaps are increased further, as a developing country, and China will face more challenges from different areas in the world during her rising.

In fact, at present, China has been entering an international friction period. According to relevant scholars, it is estimated that this friction period will last for at least 20 years. This friction is not accidental but inevitable. It is not tactical but strategic (Zhao, 2012). Given this, on the one hand, China needs to resolve international hostility through dialogue and exchange. At the same time, China must also adhere to tit-for-tat, halting and daring to struggle on the issues of the national interests. In this regard, Deng Xiaoping, China's second-generation leadership core, did an excellent job. He did well in the use of struggle strategies. When Deng Xiaoping talked about "One Country, Two Systems" and the issue of peaceful reunification of Taiwan in October 1984, he said in a clear-cut manner: The use of force must not be easy because China must concentrate on industrial construction and solve the overall problem via non-injury methods in the process of reunification (Liu, 2008).

However, China cannot give up the use of force, China must keep this in mind when using power, and this is a strategic consideration for the next generation (Deng, 1993). This perfect strategic concept of Deng Xiaoping has led us to guide our overall diplomatic activities. In the face of the complicated and volatile international situation, China cannot limit the ways to the simple practice of achieving a peaceful rise of the country by dialogue, consultation and cooperation, as it will restrict the Chinese people's thoughts and hands and will lose the struggle strategies, thus will also narrow the road to peaceful rise. The world is already full of contradictions and conflicts. China, a "huge creature" with a population of 1.4 billion, whose growth will inevitably bring about a tremendous impact on the existing international system and the world pattern, will surely arouse the suspicion and anxiety of the west and the surrounding countries. In this regard, China emphasizes that she should eliminate misunderstandings through consultation and dialogue and promotes joint development through cooperation. However, in the face of aggressive opponents, China cannot compromise blindly. The Chinese People must protect the national red line and carry out tit-for-tat struggles if necessary. Even the force can be used to promote the dialogue and correct the cooperation (Wallace and Norton, 2014).

In the face of the new challenges, all countries in the world should go beyond the traditional concepts, follow the trend of the times, strengthen exchanges and cooperation among the nations, seek common ground while reserving differences, coordinate and cooperate closely. China should push forward the world multi-polarization and the democratization of international relations actively through "One Belt One Road" construction, strive to establish a new international economic order that meets the requirements of each country, reform the irrational global financial and trade system and guarantee the equal development of all nations, especially the developing countries.

China's "One Belt One Road" strategy runs through the Asian and European continent and realizes the pluralistic, autonomous, balanced and sustainable development of all countries along the line. The strategy is not only a national policy to adapt to fit in the new changes in the world situation, but also conforms to the trend of the regional economic cooperation and global development of the world economy. The "One Belt One Road," with the spirit of open regional cooperation, is committed to safeguarding the global free trade system and the open world economy. The proposal and implementation of this strategy demonstrate that China is on the rise. As the world's largest developing country, China's international status is changing, which conforms to the fundamental interests of the international community and adds new positive energy to world peace and development.

China should respect the diversity of the developments and civilizations in various countries, and all kinds of enlightenment, all types of development paths should coexist to make up for their deficiencies in the competition and make progress together in seeking common ground while reserving differences. To establish a just and reasonable new international political and economic order, let us make active efforts to achieve lasting peace and universal prosperity in the world (Wouters and Ramopoulos, 2012).

Chapter 7
Challenges vs. Opportunities

Can China become No.1? This question was put forward shortly after the worldwide financial tsunami crisis took placed in 2008. The development of China's economy has witnessed remarkable progress in recent years, especially its unique ability to resolve the financial tsunami. In September 2009, the former assistant principal, as well as the Dean of Guanghua College of Peking University, Professor Zhang Weiying, stressed with high confidence that after the financial tsunami, it is now impossible to rely on export to stimulate economic growth. However, China's economy can still maintain its rapid growth. It may even replace the United States in the next 30 years and become the most significant economic entity in the world. Although the total economic output in China was only No.3 in the world at that time, but will the situation change in the next two years (Yu, 2018)?

Introduction

On April 7, 2011, the Social Science Press conducted a seminar titled "Rise of BRICS and Global Development and Governance" in Beijing and a press conference on the "Blue Book for Emerging Economies" in Beijing. This conference discussed the developments and changes in emerging economies and the new trend of global development and governance reform. At this conference, A Blue Book of Emerging Economies titled the BRICS Economic and Social Development Report (2011) was formally released. In this Blue Book, it predicted that China's total economic output may surpass the United States by 2020, and then will rank first in the world, while India's GDP will list the world's top five (Lin and Zhou, 2011).

This cannot convince the people of the world. The International Monetary Fund once predicted in 2011 that the proportion of the United

States and China in the world economy would also change by 2016. China's percentage would increase from 14% then to 18% in 2016, while the United States would drop from slightly below 20% to 17.7% in 2016, which would be lower than China a little bit and thus be the second in the world. Of course, the International Monetary Fund is not the first one to make such a prediction. Nobel laureate Fogel predicted that China would become the world's largest economy by 2020 (Chang, 2017).

A UK magazine Economist published a monograph about the assumption that China and the United States would have 7.75% and 2.5% GDP growth respectively over the next ten years, with inflation rates of 4% and 1.5%. China's GDP would surpass the United States by 2019. At the same time, World Bank economists predicted that China's economy would overtake the United States and the EU in 2030 and become the world's largest economic market. By that time, China, the United States, the European Union, India, Japan would change behavior like "five dragons" to promote the world economy. In fact, many foreign agencies had predicted whether China's economy would exceed the United States or not (Yin and Yang, 2011).

Although, as a matter of fact, some of the above estimation and predictions were realized, and some were not realized, there is no doubt that China's economy has kept growing. According to China's official statistics, China's economic development continues to strengthen, with its gross domestic product exceeding 90 trillion yuan in 2018, equivalent to 13.4 trillion US dollars. In the 2018 GDP ranking of relevant countries in the world, China firmly ranks second in the world, 67% of the United States, and 16% of the world's total GDP (see Table 7.1).

Table 7.1 GDP Ranking of Relevant Countries in the World in 2018

Ranking	Country	Billion (USD)	Increase of over 2017 (%)
1	United States	205802.5	2.927
2	China	133680.73	6.567
3	Japan	49717.67	1.940
4	Germany	39513.40	1.522
5	Britain	28288.33	1.398
6	France	27801.52	1.725
7	India	27187.32	6.811
8	Italy	20758.56	0.858
9	Brazil	18678.18	1.114
10	Canada	17124.79	1.879

The data comes from the IMF official website.

Can China become No.1 or not? This is an objective question. We need to consider the actual situation in China. In conditions where opportunities and challenges coexist, are chances more than challenges? Or challenge more than the opportunities? This will affect the question. Besides, we must also consider the history of China, such as the origin of China's peaceful rise. Since ancient times, China is a peace-loving country and has always adhered to such diplomacy as "not seeking hegemony." Well, one of the questions we are discussing is, "can China be No.1?" Is this contrary to the national guidelines and policies? This needs a thorough discussion. Finally, as Chinese scholars indicate that we also need to consider a subjective question: Does China want to be No.1? Just like the "demand" that occurred in economics, people must have the willingness to buy first, then the purchasing power, to become a real "need" eventually. When we talk about whether China can become the world leader or not, the truth is the same. Therefore, only when both subjectivity and objective have been reached, can we conclude (Cheng, 2017).

Can China Rise peacefully?

"One Belt One Road" strategy is of great strategic importance for China to continue to enter the world and continue to integrate into the world. From the international background, the United States, especially after President Trump came to power, suddenly realized that China has become bigger, and the potential threat to the US hegemony is greater. In particular, today's increasingly powerful China has neither collapsed as predicted by the mainstream Chinese School in the United States nor has it become more and more like the United States as predicted by the non-mainstream school in the United States. Therefore, both schools are in a hurry and think that the United States needs to take action to deal with China's peaceful rise, so as not to pose a growing strategic threat to the United States. This is the main background for the United States to launch a trade war with China. Most Chinese scholars now predict that in 2021, whether Donald Trump, or Joseph Robinette Biden, or anyone else will take office, the United States will carry out a policy of repression against China. It can be imagined that if the United States and Japan can do a good job in Europe at the same time, then China will be in a very dangerous strategic situation. "One Belt One Road" is China's strategy to tackle China's military balance, and containment through economic development. It is also crucial to ensuring China's policy of peaceful development and peaceful rise.

Dr. Zhao Jingfang is an associate professor working at the Crisis Management Center of the National Defense University. He said that China's economic strength had been enhanced continuously in these recent years. The crisis which China has encountered in the surrounding areas has been increased steadily. It is going to be more difficult for China to rise peacefully. This is a strategic environment that cannot be ignored by China. When facing the strategic situation that has changed and is still changing rapidly, we must overcome our general misunderstandings about the peaceful rise and adjust the current strategic thinking and tactics in time. This is what we must do. Only in this way will China pass the undercurrents on the broad road of peaceful development (Xu, 2017).

Undoubtedly, it will depend on not only the economic and diplomatic forces but also the military development when China rises peacefully. Therefore, it is not just the rise of economy and diplomacy, but also the growth of the military. Only relying on this kind of multiple climbs can China realize the full peaceful increase. In other words, without the support of economic and diplomatic forces, the quiet rise is hollow and false, without the guarantee of military power, the peaceful rise will be fragile and unsustainable (Zhao, 2012).

When talking about the economic development of China, the international community changed their words immediately. They disseminated various "threat theories" concerning the rise of China and even exaggerated the economic growth to the political and military levels. They believed that China would inevitably end up on the path of hegemony in the war. International historical studies on China are far from enough for those who think so. China is neither a militant nation like the United States nor a colonial expansion like Europe throughout the history of China. Even before the Opium War, China never had such a thought to keep its position of number one in the world through the war. These are inseparable from the history and culture of China (Cao, 2016).

Of course, it should be a peaceful rise, if possible. So, what is the increase? It has the meaning of accelerating national economic development. However, when we say the rise of China, where the purpose is different, the growths we are talking about means the increase of comprehensive national strength and then affect the world's forces, order and code of conduct (Yan, 1997). In the history of China, China has had her rise on several occasions: the first one was the unification of China governed by the Qin Dynasty, and this is the first unification for China; the second rise was the establishment of the Tang Dynasty, and then its flourishing life occur; the third one is the Ming Dynasty, Zheng He's voyages was the landmark event, who brought the Chinese civilization to the Middle East and North Africa. The fourth rise came to us after the Cold War (He, 2005). All these four rises are mild and friendly; thus, it is safe to say that China is a "state of ceremonies," which is not "war" or "killing" at all.

In the history of China, Confucianism that represented by Confucius, was regarded as the "golden rules" of governing the country since the Han Dynasty. At that time, people ignored all other theories except the Confucianism. Confucianism needs us to be "courtesy" and "benevolent" to govern the country; it advocated governing with virtue and gentleness. In modern society, these are just "governing the country with virtue" and "governing the country according to the laws." Nowadays, the strategy is more enlightened and equal; some bad ideas have been abandoned. One should not impose on others what he does not want; we are all good friends no matter where you live. The Chinese have known this kind of idea. The previous emperors of China also kept Confucianism as their ways to govern the nation. For example, when we see the portrait or sculpture of the last Chinese emperors, it comes to our mind immediately that they all look like people believing in Confucianism (Fan, 2018).

The political concepts are different under different civilizations, only China was never interrupted during the past 2000 years, and the Chinese nation was the only nation that did not advocate military force. In comparison, the westerners believe in the theory of the original sin of human nature. Thus they uphold the domination by law. They also advocate the "law of the jungle." The brilliance in the Roman Empire, the France domination in Europe during the Napoleonic times and the mighty United States after the Cold War, all these illustrate that Westerners have a compelling idea to dominate the citizens by the military force (Chen, 2004). There is good news that the Confucian ideology and culture represented by Confucius, is moving into the world and being accepted by more and more countries in the world under the current complicated cultural background, which is helpful to bring human beings into a peaceful and new era (Huang, 2017).

In the contemporary era, the Chinese are more likely to fall into a perceptual way of thinking. That is, they explain the international relations and diplomatic strategies according to the western model.

They stubbornly believe that it is a normal phenomenon to struggle for supremacy. Because the Westerners are thinking: you are already so powerful, why not go seeking hegemony? They think it is unbelievable and weird for a country if not to go exploring authority after becoming powerful (Hou, 2018).

However, Chinese leaders have continuously declared that this way of thinking should be given up. For example, on December 10, 2003, Wen Jiabao, the Chinese Premier, then held a speech entitled "Investing in China" at Harvard University. This is the first time that Wen Jiabao represented the Chinese government and explained the theory of China's peaceful rise to the world publicly and transparently. In that speech, he said that China is a country that is rising peacefully. In his speech, Wen Jiabao also pointed out that the path, mode and value orientation during China's rise will be based on peace. This is the first time that the top Chinese leaders use the phrase "peaceful rise," which marks China's peaceful rise as a fundamental national strategy (Zhang and Jiang, 2011). Since then, the Chinese leadership has addressed the same in various situations in the international community.

On July 1, 2016, President Xi Jinping declared at the celebration of the 95th anniversary of the Chinese Communist Party: We hope to promote the relationships with all other countries, to help to establish a new type of international relations under the win-win cooperation and to encourage the formation for human destinies community and benefits community. The human destinies community will not only bring benefits to China but also the world. China's development and strength are not threats but opportunities for other countries. At the j 19th Chinese Communist Party Congress, Xi Jinping appealed once again that all people in the world should work together to build a community of human destiny and to establish a world of lasting peace, universal security, shared prosperity, inclusiveness, cleanliness and beauty (Li, 2017).

China is a sincere country and is ready to develop with all other countries in the world in a prosperous manner. "One Belt One Road" strategy is the best proof. "One Belt One Road" refers to the principle that we must uphold our everyday business and build our beautiful life together and then share it. It is not a soloist of a particular country, but a chorus of the countries along the line. When rising peacefully, China also allows other states to get on the "free bus" to support the joint development of all nations and to build a shared garden (Ma, 2017).

Chinese people believe that the rise and development of China will not threaten any country or any people. They insist that if some countries or some people in the world still support the "China threat theory," the Chinese had better ask them whether they should return to the poor and weak era and return to the humiliation era when all others were attacking them. Is this what you meant? Is this what you recognized as "safe"? If so, where is the fairness of the world going? "If one can be stable in all his life, nobody would want to be displaced." This sentence is particularly suitable to show China's current situation. The Chinese people are peace-loving and dislike of the war, which has been handed down from generation to generation and cannot be changed in the future. Moreover, the Chinese are quite happy to continue like before (Qiu and Zhao, 2017).

Some Chinese scholars indicate that: when we cannot rise peacefully and when our rise is suppressed, we cannot and will not give up our rise. In other words, if we are unable to rise peacefully, we will also consider different ways. Therefore, for China, apart from the strategic thinking for growing peacefully, the most important thing is to find whether we have the strength and ability to rise peacefully, that is, whether we will have enough military power when the wars happen. They claimed that China's military power would become more durable and more reliable, and it is impossible for the Western countries headed by the United States to attack China to guarantee the stability thoroughly around the neighboring areas (Zhao, 2012).

The theoretical model of the three components of GDP termed as "troika" of pulling forces for macro economies by the Chinese scholars is a deformation of the Keynesian short-term analysis framework (Shen 2009). Keynes put forward the "effective demand" theory in "General Theory of Employment, Interest, and Money," which is when the aggregate demand with the capacity to pay the aggregate supply and then the total demand reach equilibrium. The overall economic volume consists of four aspects: total residents' consumption, total investment, government expenditure, and net exports, while the proportion of government expenditure is limited (Keynes 2018). Therefore, consumption, investment, and export are the three components of GDP compared to the "troika" driving economic development. In different periods of economic development, various aspects of the "troika" play different roles in driving economic development, and the resulting "troika" theory of economic growth naturally reflects consumer demand, investment demand, and export demand (Muellbauer and Lattimore 1995). The short-term analysis framework of the three components of GDP can well represent the driving force of traditional economic growth.

Different theorists have different opinions. There is no definite answer. However, this is positive that it has never been said that the wagon "consumption" is the main force driving the growth of China's economy. Therefore, China's future economic development opportunities will emerge in consumption. In recent years, what China has always emphasized is to stimulate domestic demand while growing stably. However, where does the most significant part of domestic demand come from? Consumers in China can be grouped into two smaller ones at the two ends and a big one in the middle, while the middle one will serve as the principal breakthrough forces to increase the domestic demand (Cai, 2016).

Nowadays, the people in the middle class do not consume too much; where did the money go? Let us take a look at China's CPI. It is well known that the money will be devalued if you just put it in the bank. Such a small savings rate simply cannot make up for the current inflation losses. Where did the money of people in the middle class go? Would it not go away? Even though the wage level is not high, but it is enough to maintain a livelihood, why the consumption is not very active? It is not difficult to find out the reasons. Let us look at education, which is the most significant spending for general working-class people.

Nowadays the education has become entirely different from what it was before; it has been "commercialized." Not to mention all kinds of malpractices in China's education system, one can have a look at the education fees. The tuitions and expenses that a high school student pays are as high as dozens of thousands. Education should be one of the public welfare, but it has now become a tool for profit. Chinese citizens have nothing to do but to tighten their belts, not to spend money on other stuff anymore, just for their children's education, and thus they live frugally, except this, what else can they do (Zheng, 2017)?

Let us look at China's real estate, which is more severe than education. A house is just a place for people to live in, but in China, people buy homes and then sell them to make money. Those real estate investors or speculators, they may say: China's stock market is not making money. If you do not buy a house, where will you put your money? Finally, let us look at social security. Everyone may get sick and die. This is unavoidable. The people in the middle class must prepare for their post-retirement living arrangements, especially in the face of catastrophic illness, which will make it even more troublesome if there is not enough money available. After considering the above three points, for most people, most of the savings they made in their whole life are now empty, with no further money to spend on other consumption. What to talk about domestic demand? Even if you have a need, but if you do not have the ability, it is useless. Therefore, the middle-class, there will be some potentiality that can be exploited; it will become a fantastic opportunity for China's economic development. This depends on the actions taken by those policymakers (Zhang, 2017).

In addition to the working-class people, there is another large group that we cannot ignore, that is the peasants' group. China is a big agricultural country. The "three rural issues (agriculture, farming and peasants)" are what China has been trying to improve, and they have achieved remarkable results. To increase the peasants' income, this is another important measure for the CPC Central Committee to stimulate domestic demand. Moreover, accelerating urbanization will also help to increase the revenue of Chinese peasants. During their spare time, peasants will find opportunities to work in the nearby town or county. This is so-called “migrant workers.” This group has a crucial role in urbanization. By perfecting the household registration system and employment system gradually, urbanization will go faster! It was said that China’s urbanization lags far behind the industrialization, so there will be a variety of “labor shortage.” Then, this “shortage” is going to be another historical opportunity for China’s economic development (Mao, 2017).

If China wants its economy to develop further, it is not enough to rely on the hard power GDP solely. Therefore, the soft power culture will be served as a critical role while promoting economic development. In the late 1980s, the dean of Kennedy Political Science School at Harvard University, Professor Joseph S. Nye Jr., found that the soft and hard power of the United States is not symmetrical among its overall strength, which is harmful to the United States. Then the concept of soft power was put forward strategically. China paid close attention to this kind of soft power theory. Chinese scholars and politicians agreed with the basic argument of Joseph Nye and accepted it congruously. They decided that culture is an essential source of soft power, and it also served as a significant role during the development of a country. Nye believed that the causes of soft power are also continually expanding as time goes on. For example, in this era of internet information, how to master and control the information? This kind of ability is also crucial for a country’s soft power (Wang, 1993; Ni, 2001).

It is quite unbalanced between different regions for China’s economic and social development. It is developed much better in the eastern area than in the western area. According to the statistics, it covers over 60% of the country’s large cities, industrial production bases and export processing bases within 200 kilometers of the coast in China’s eastern region. The coastal population in the east accounted for 36.1% of China’s total. From 1979 to 2008, it absorbed 81.2% of the total foreign direct investments in our country. From 2005 to 2008, the regional GDP accounted for an average of 55.6% of China’s total, while the industrial added value accounted for 59.8%, Total exports accounted for about 89% (Ji, 2011).

In 2009, the GDP of 11 provinces and municipalities on the eastern coast accounted for nearly 60% of the national total. In contrast, economic and social development in the western region will be much worse. According to the statistics, 12 provinces, individual cities and autonomous territories in the part of the west of China account for about one-third of the population of the country and 71% of the land area. However, due to natural, historical and social reasons, the economic development in the western region lags. Per capita GDP is only equivalent to two-thirds of the national average and less than 40% of the average level in the eastern region. The western part not only has a large population but also has abundant resources and excellent market potential. Its strategic position is essential. To speed up the economic and social development in the western region and bring its economic and social development at or near the eastern region level is undoubtedly a massive economy for China Development Opportunities (Ji, 2011).

The soft power culture in China can be said to be a "fertile soil" to be excavated. If it is effectively used, it can be transformed into a powerful real productive force. The value created by the American cultural industry has already exceeded the total amount of heavy industry and light industry. How can Chinese culture go to the world? Some scholars have elaborated on the grandness and limitations of Chinese culture completely and provide some concrete opinions on the developments and constructions of China's cultural soft power (Sun, 2018).

It is far from enough to reply on its internal strength alone for developing China's economy. Under such a global trend, the development of a country is inextricably linked to the world environment. Undoubtedly, peace and development are the main themes for the current time. Therefore, the external environment for China's future economic growth will still be favorable. Although there are the hegemony and threat from the United States, the global public opinion is still justice. If the United States wants to act willfully, all the people in the world will not agree. Even the native citizens of the United States oppose the war; after all, no one wants to live a tense day in the war (Chen, 2014).

As for the opportunities for China's economic development, the above enumeration is not complete or comprehensive, and we have never thought of enumerating it endlessly. In short, only when the internal and external environment meets the development needs, can economic development be better. However, the fact is usually not satisfactory. Everything does not exist entirely. Therefore, after talking about the opportunities for China's economic development, the following discussion will undoubtedly concern the challenge of China's economic growth. This is a stereotype, but it is also necessary to solve issues completely. After all, every coin has two sides, and one cannot see the trees out of the woods, which makes the taboo of academia (Fan, 2017).

Challenges of China's economic development

Since we are talking about the challenges for China's economic development, let us skip those issues that are common to the entire world for a long time and let us talk about China's unique challenges with Chinese characteristics mainly. Only in this way can we know the gaps between China and the world more clearly and honestly and answer the question of whether China can become No.1 (Fu, 2016).

China's administrative interventionism is an embarrassing economic phenomenon. Admittedly, this authoritarianism is quite beneficial to economic development in certain aspects and can make up for market defects. Of course, in a fully market-oriented economy, we must pay more attention to the rules of the market and appropriately reduce administrative interference. The experience told us that an economic development model characterized by an authoritarian system might be useful in completing financial accumulation. However, as a non-balanced development model, it also pays a heavy toll on economic achievements. Such imbalances are short-term behavior of economic development, the disparity between rich and poor, corruption, and civil rights issues. To be specific, the government represents some people's benefits in some ways and most of these people that already benefited serve as officials. It is harmful to the market economy development (Chen and Ren, 2015).

There will be a series of internal problems with Chinese characteristics once the economy involves politics and power, and it is easy for the corruption to be turned up and generated by using the national authority for private benefits. In China, all people know the real meaning of the word "relationship," however, it may be unfamiliar for those foreigners, who do not know the actual meaning of this unique word used by Chinese people, but Chinese people have a clear understanding. This is not intended to belittle or ridicule people. Instead, the Chinese want to warn or remind them that the market economy will exert its unique charm by reducing unnecessary administrative interference.

Of course, the reduction does not mean complete elimination. Necessary macroeconomic regulation and control are indispensable. A few years ago, it turned out to be an uproar for Guangzhou Pharmaceutical regarding the Jiaduobao and Wanglaoji trademarks, because Guangzhou Pharmaceutical is a state-owned enterprise. At the same time, Jiaduobao is a private enterprise, and finally, the brand was given to Guangzhou Pharmaceutical according to the concerning laws. Otherwise, there would be a loss for state-owned assets. Professor Lang Xianping pointed out that "this is a win-win thing, Jiaduobao produces Red Pot Wanglaoji, and Guangzhou Pharmaceutical produces Green Box Wanglaoji, but now it became a zero-sum game. If all acts in favor of the state-owned enterprises, who would dare to go with the none state-owned enterprises in the future?" This issue is worth pondering. It is going to be imperative to change government functions (Heng, 2017).

The administrative interventionism is a phenomenon in current China known as "official standard," which functions as a major hindrance to China's economic development. It is not very accurate to term it, but it is really a major obstacle, a "cancer" that affects social fairness and justice. Of course, the thought "official standard" has its historical reasons. The traditional Chinese ideology that lasts for more than 2,000 years is one of the reasons. When talking about the "official standard," some people say it is a kind of consciousness, some think it is a kind of culture, some think it is an ideology, and others define it differently. The meanings of "official standard" are referring the following two points: one is the official-oriented consciousness existing in people's minds, and the other is the official-oriented phenomenon driven by the official awareness (zhu and Bei,2008).

In their minds, the officials' benefits are over all others. They protect the interests of officials at the beginning and in the end. Fortunately, what we advocate now is "people-oriented" rather than "official-oriented." When the day comes, Chinese people will no longer be forced to demolish their houses, and private rights will no longer be misused. The people can accuse officials with no difficulties. By that time, China's "people-based standard" will be corrected indeed.

When speaking about China's economy, we must talk about China's real estate, because a large part of China's economy comes from the real estate market, this phenomenon is just like: one piece of hair gets pulled, and then the whole body will be affected. The necessary regulation for the real estate market cannot be relaxed. Otherwise, it is very likely to cause real estate blowout. On the face of it, China's real estate is so hot because of its large population and its scarcity. It is wrong to look at the problem if we just look at the appearance without seeing the inside. China has a vast territory, and it is straightforward to realize that let our Chinese residents have their own houses. However, the housing problem is so severe in China. The housing system problems are just the reasons. The "restriction order" issued by China's government is the best remedy for it (Ma, 2017).

Since ancient times, the Chinese have been paying attention to settling down for their lives. The house is a recognized "symbol of stability." For most people, the house represents a kind of security. Under the guidance of such ideas, China's rich people started to buy homes madly and made money by selling houses. Then those "house slaves," who were mostly working-class people who would suffer finally. As a result, the polarization will be accelerated even further. The rich will use the real estate to seek more benefits, and the poor will have to pay a higher price for it. The most important thing is to control the real estate market strictly to compress the real estate bubble, thus return to economic development rationality. At the same time, the laws supporting real estate should also be further improved. Only when the legislation and law enforcement instruments are built, will the economy not be in ups and downs so that a country can move forward at a stable speed (Tang, 2017).

Compared with the American economy, most of China's economy relies on the material economy. The development potential of the material economy is minimal. It does not have a substantially vertical and horizontal extension like the virtual economy. Some of China's economy has been exploited and plundered by the virtual economy from the United States. Why do we say so? You can have a look at China's development model, "manufacturing power," "Made in China," which means China is a country that produces physical products. Still, the United States owns the virtual economy, such as named brands, intellectual properties and so on, plus her innovative technologies, as well as the monopoly of the United States dollars, so the US will be able to gain the benefits with ease. Therefore, China still has a long way to go in terms of a virtual economy.

It is both an opportunity and a challenge for China to speed up international exchanges and expand the economy abroad. At present, China has set up more than 12,000 overseas direct investment enterprises in 174 countries and regions, with a total number of over 4 million overseas workers. In 2009, China used a total of 90.03 billion U.S. dollars of foreign capital, and its exports amounted to 1.216 trillion U.S. dollars, ranking the first in the world. In 2011, China imported 254 million tons of crude oil. At the same time, China's overseas investments are still increasing. China's economic development is significantly dependent on offshore resources and markets. Therefore, if China cannot protect foreign assets, international energy, and trade channels, and overseas workers effectively, China's economic development and the economic benefits will be challenged profoundly (Zhao, 2012).

To promote the overall open pattern and perfect the system of China's foreign trade is crucial to the opening of our country at this stage. President Xi Jinping proposed at the 19th National Congress that we shall focus on the "One Belt and One Road" construction, stick to the principle "building and sharing jointly," adhere to the policy "co-construction and sharing," and strengthen openness and cooperation, expand foreign trade and foster a new model of trade format. It is necessary for China to change the ways of overseas investment, to promote international cooperation in production capacity, to form a global business, finance, production, and service network, and to accelerate training international economic cooperation and competition. Only by keeping pace with the outward expansion of the economy, will China's foreign economy and the people's interests be protected. This is also a significant problem that needs to be paid attention to at the present stage of international trade.

As for the question, "Can China become No.1 or not?" In addition to talking about the advantages of China, it is also necessary to ask the current No.1, which is the United States. The formidable opponent will undermine the competitiveness of China's economic development. The United States is a country with vast natural resources. The US has the third-largest land area in the world, the fourth largest forest area in the world, the fifth largest land available per capita in the world, the 12th largest proven oil reserve in the world, ranking the fifth in the world and the coal reserve ranks first in the world. Moreover, the US attitude to China's economic development will also affect the external development environment.

U.S. policy toward China hardened during the second Obama Administration and has become more hostile since Donald Trump took power in Washington. Four factors may be causing this drastic change: (1) the shifting of power between the two countries in favor of China; (2) increased ideological differences between them; (3) conflicting economic interests; and (4) China is seen as a scapegoat in U.S. domestic politics. While a combination of the four factors can help explain the transformation of U.S. policy, the author argues that the changing behavior of China in the recent decade has been more influential in reshaping U.S. attitudes. The China–U.S. relationship may further deteriorate in the coming years, but observers are hopeful that the two giants can avoid violent confrontation.

On June 5, 2012, the United States published the "Report on the Development of Military Power in China." On June 16 and 18, 2012, China's Shenzhou Ninth satellite got launched and docked with a Tiangong satellite. This brought concern in the United States, Japan, and South Korea and a new round of "China threat" argument. Another example: In 2015, China led the establishment of the Asian Infrastructure Investment Bank (AIIB), which was established to promote the interoperability and economic integration in Asia and to strengthen the cooperation between China and other Asian countries and regional cooperation. The foreign media distorted it as the Chinese version of the "Marshall Plan." Besides, to defend its supremacy, the United States suppressed the development of China. In Obama's presidency, the United States reached a Trans-Pacific Partnership agreement (TPP) with 12 countries such as Japan and Australia etc. and set a series of rules and conditions for China to stop China from joining.

When Donald Trump took over the power, he withdrew from the TPP and launched a trade war with China. In action, the Trump administration has launched all-out confrontational activities against China, including initiating the trade war; undermining Chinese high-tech enterprises represented by Huawei Technologies, restricting bilateral educational, scientific and technological and cultural exchanges with China; stepping up "freedom of navigation" operations in the South China Sea; strengthening defense cooperation with Asia–Pacific countries such as Japan, India, and Australia aimed at China; designing and operating what Washington calls the strategy of "a free and open Indo-Pacific" (U.S. Department of Defense 2019); dispatching high-ranking officials for political and military exchanges with the

Taiwan authorities; selling advanced weaponry to Taiwan; and supporting Hong Kong's "peaceful demonstrations" and protests that Beijing censures. The U.S. Department of Justice created a "China initiative" task force to crack down on alleged espionage (U.S. Department of Justice 2019). In November 2019, President Trump signed the "Hong Kong Human Rights and Democracy Act of 2019" passed by Congress. The enforcement of this Act may seriously hamper China's interests (Wang, 2020).

More recently, the United States began eliminating Hong Kong's special status under U.S. law on Monday, halting defense exports and restricting the territory's access to high technology products as China prepares new Hong Kong security legislation. The U.S. move comes as the top decision-making body of China's parliament deliberates a draft national security law for Hong Kong that pro-democracy activists in the city fear will be used to eliminate dissent and tighten Beijing's control. It can be said precisely because of the irreconcilability between China and the western countries that China cannot obtain the identity of the "peaceful rise" in the international community no matter how it is advocated (Zhao, 2012).

In addition to the challenges discussed above, China also has the following problems such as the population aging, extensive economic growth, employment issues, and the loss of cheap labor. All these problems will affect the future development of China's economy, and China needs to change its methods for economic growth, to strengthen independent innovation, to improve the employment system, to think of ways to avoid the loss of cheap labor.

The temptation to become No.1

Why do all countries in the world strive to become economic powers, and want to become the dominant global economy like the United States? Of course, because it is full of temptations to become No.1, it will own the economic power that other countries cannot catch up with. Otherwise, who would be so stupid to be the Number One in the world (Wang and Zhu, 2017)?

The United States financial hegemony brought enormous benefits to the Americans and has surpassed the benefits gained from the real economic growth in the United States. This is mainly due to the dominance of the U.S. dollar. Because the U.S. dollar is the world currency, products from all over the world can be bought with green papers issued by the United States. Also, the government can get money globally by issuing U.S. bonds and trading American company stocks. And this is only a string of numb figures for the United States, which is increased by this means. The United States has always been very clear about its liabilities because this will in no way affect the U.S. economy. The United States has ever interfered with the exchange rate of Japanese Yen through its U.S. dollar supremacy. The "Plaza Accord" is the testimony.

A "conspiracy" with regards to the Yen appreciation has caused Japan's economy to be unstable. All the countries today are worried whether their domestic currencies will be the next "target" or not. A couple of nations led by the United States are asking for the appreciation of the Renminbi, which seems to imply that these developed countries are doing the same as what they did before once again. China still can say no currently, but who can guarantee that China's economy can always say no to power? After all, economic strength is the most important thing! Without industrial strength, we can only live in miserable conditions where people are pauperized. Given the enormous benefits like the dollar's monopoly, will the Renminbi become the next world currency? We can only wait and see (Xia, 2018).

In addition to the economic benefits brought by the world currency U.S. dollar, the United States economic hegemony can also affect the rights and prestige of international financial organizations. The United States never denies its "double standard" in terms of the trade policy. On the one hand, the United States has no scruples in giving trade subsidies to its disadvantaged industries. On the other hand, the United States insists on applying anti-subsidy barriers to its trading partners. Although this "pendulum" trade policy of the United States brought about some loss, it obtained lots of "relative interests" when it suppressed the opponent countries. This hegemony strategy that looked like "Kill 1,000 enemies and 800 self-losses" guaranteed the U.S. economic interests, and the position as the world economic leader was kept (Cheng, 2005).

The United States is more afraid than any other country to be surpassed and fears that its economic hegemony will not be guaranteed because the US knows all kinds of "sweetness" brought about by economic domination. The supremacy strategies and tactics of the United States differ at various stages and in different fields. However, it can be summed up as follows: to lead the world through establishing universal international organizations; to control the global economy under the banner of national self-determination and trade liberalization; to avoid direct colonial rule but to rule the entire world; to maintain its financial dominance by keeping the hegemony via issuing dollars (Li, 2009).

In the international arena, the United States has always acted as the "world policeman." In a sense, the United States plays a significant role in establishing and maintaining the international order, although this order is unfair and flawed. Therefore, to perfect the new economic order, it requires more economic discourse power, China must speak in strength! The world economy follows the law of the jungle as well. This rule is the so-called survival of the fittest.

Chinese authorities always oppose hegemonies and power politics, but here we are talking about the No.1 in the economic area, and this is different from political domination. It is recognized widely that economic hegemony can bring economic benefits to its own country, especially in formulating and operating the economic system. No matter China's economy can become the leader in the world or not, what China needs is to have a natural result, excluding all the other abnormal ways. Even in the face of such an enormous temptation, China still must abide by the guidelines for economic development. As for the world leader, we shall think of it like this: "It is my luck if I own it, while it is my fate if I lose it."

Both China and America are undergoing dramatic domestic transformation, the direction of which will determine whether, and how, they can find a way to rehabilitate the links that have benefited the two countries over the last 40 years. China is changing more rapidly than America and will continue to change at its own pace and on its chosen path. To dodge a potentially fatal confrontation, the two countries should engage each other in good competition to facilitate satisfied and just societies and earn the respect of the rest of the world (Wang, 2020).

Can China be No.1?

After a series of questions have been discussed, another issue we want to know is: Can China become No.1? According to the current development situation in China and the international situation, China has some primary conditions to become the No.1, but it is not sufficient. Therefore, we think China can become the No.1, but not now, maybe soon. There will be all kinds of pressure in addition to enjoying a variety of benefits after being the No.1. Therefore, to become the No.1 is not as easy as what one can think. The pies will not be fallen from the sky. This principle is well known by the world leader (Zhang, 2017).

"One Belt One Road" initiative was proposed to be the most important strategy for China to be the No. 1. For the Chinese people and nation, it is a great strategy for China to break away from the unequal international trade negotiations led by the US and seek broader strategies for resources and market cooperation. This is the first time that China has put forward the framework of intercontinental development and cooperation with China as the leading force in the past 200 years. The implementation and success of this strategy will completely break away from the geopolitical situation of relying on big countries and being attacked passively. It has great historical and practical significance for China to become a world-class power.

However, there must be a price to pay to become the No.1, and sometimes the cost is exceptionally high. The financial crisis in the United States can be regarded as potential harm caused by its economic hegemon. Only when it has been accumulated slowly will it erupt, and its power will exceed the normal economic scope. After becoming the No.1, it will be more challenging to maintain. This is so-called "It is easy to fight for sovereignty over rivers and mountains, but it is difficult to keep it from being robbed again." Think about it carefully and deeply, does China still want to become the No.1? Napoleon has ever said, "Soldiers who do not want to be generals are not good soldiers." For China, the development of the economy should not be disturbed too much by human factors whether China can become the No.1 or not, which is not controlled by one or two.

It is not so easy and as fast as we think if China wants to overtake the United States or replace the United States as the world's economic No.1. For now, China still needs to move forward stably under the world economic order led by the United States. Only by doing so can China devotes all its efforts to development. In recent years, the United States has helped China a little bit on economic growth. After all, the United States has maintained a relatively stable space for China. From this point of view, the United States is still quite "authentic" (Zou, 2017).

In the face of the topic, "When will China overtake the United States?" the most appropriate attitude should be talking more about the issues and less about catch-up, having more senses of worry and less pride, having more reasons to go ahead with reform and innovation and less self-defending. Sometimes, intentionally planted flowers would not blossom; unintentional plated trees would be grown up rapidly. All Chinese people know this truth very well.

China, as a traditional East Asian country, it is understandable that China wants to regain its position as an enormous power during the peaceful rise of China. However, if it is going to be excluded or suppressed by other countries, the reason is that the other states are considering whether China will become a king or a hegemon, and bring peace or war to the world. Perhaps when we return to that part, "the peaceful rise of China's economy," the Chinese people will have a clear and definite answer.

As indicated in our preface and it is necessary to repeat that the One Belt One Road initiative not only enhanced the fast development of China but also generated an impact on the world's political and economic patterns. Some American political leaders believe that China's aggressive and robust rise is to replace the United States' leading position in the world. However, some Chinese scholars believe that in China, there may be a very few, but absolutely not dominant, among the top leaders think so, and this idea does not have any realistic possibility. The reasons are as follows: first, Chinese is not the international language; second, RMB is not an international currency; third, China cannot deliver military power to the world; fourth, China cannot provide a series of public goods to the world; fifth, most countries in the world do not recognize China's current system and values, as such there is no real ally for China; sixth, China's economy ranks second in the world in terms of appearance and essence, the dazzling total amount divided by 1.4 billion denominators will rank behind in the world; seventh, the contradictions accumulated in China's rapid growth in recent decades are mostly suppressed by "maintaining stability and have not yet been resolved. Finally, education in China is rigid and ideological suffocation leads to science and technology learning without thickness, good at imitating the first-class but poor in innovation, lack of long-distance running endurance. Therefore, China cannot be the leader of the global village (Weng, 2018).

As to the United States, Chinese scholars believe that the United States is at the peak of its development, and it usually goes downhill when it reaches its peak. However, the peak of the United States is not mounting Everest, but it is in a flat top of the mountain. It may take a long time for the United States to go through this flat top of the mountain. Therefore, the United States can continue to be the leader of the world. However, the United States also has two key issues to pay attention to: first, the United States may not replace international law with its domestic law; second, the United States should consult with others when there are somethings must be done, and it is better not to act arbitrarily (Weng, 2018).

In conclusion, China, as the largest developing country and an emerging world economic leader, has sufficient resources, financial resources and industries to carry out the "One Belt One Road" initiative and assure its success. Moreover, the "One Belt One Road" initiative is a bright prospect for the future world depicted by the Chinese leadership under the background of world multi-polarization and economic globalization. This bright prospect has attracted many countries to participate actively. The initiative has provided many better channels and ways for infrastructure development and economic development for many developing countries, and it has opened up new avenues for better cooperation among countries. Therefore, this initiative is bound to be strongly supported by all countries in the world who want to develop friendly relations and better develop their economy based on win-win cooperation. Especially, as the world economies have been severely impacted by the pandemic of Covid-19, while China has successfully controlled the continuously expending of the pandemic and accumulated experiences and materials, China must work with the world, particularly with the countries that have involved in the One Belt One Road initiative to recover the economies after the pandemic. Therefore, this initiative is bound to succeed.

Bibliography

Abramson, J. and Hollingshead, C. (2009). Marketing on the Internet: Providing Consumer Satisfaction. Journal of Internet Marketing, Vol. 2009 (1): 1.

Ali Research Institute (2017). Report on Five Forecasts for Netrepreneur Report 2017.

Analysis Framework, Generation Mechanism and Governance Strategy, 2017(03): 131-136.

Bai, Bin, and Zhang Zaisheng. (2017). Political Cost of Environmental Problems:

Bandiwadekar, D. (2002). Internet marketing: International marketing using trading portals and search engines. Marketing Educator, Vol.2002 (20): 2.

Bao, Hong and Bi, Fangning. (2016). A strategic conception of "one belt and one road" under the perspective of Marx doctrine. Motherland, 2016 (15): 116-117.

Bi, Jiankang (1992). The Impact of the Marshall Plan on Western European Economy. American Studies, 1992 (4): 87-103.

Cai, Fang (2016). How does China give impetus to global economic growth? The People's Congress of China, 2016 (21):13-14.

Cao, Yifeng and Xue, Jun (2006). An Overview of Research on Online Consumer Behavior. Market Modernization, Vol. 2006 (477).

Cao, Zheng (2016). Misunderstanding of Democracy: Comments by foreign scholars on China's authoritarianism. Reform & Opening. 453 (24): 39-42.

Ceparano, Maria Carmela, and Quartieri Federico. 2017. Nash equilibrium uniqueness in nice games with isotone best replies. Journal of Mathematical Economics, 2017,70.

Chang, Zheng (2017). The rise of China is different from the United States and Japan. Leadership Science, 2017 (29): 61-64.

Chen Jiang-Sheng, Tian Miao (2017). The formation, implementation and influence of The Belt and Road Initiative. CPC History Studies, 2017(02): 5-13.

Chen, Hanwen (1985). In the International Arena. Chengdu, PRC: Sichuan People's Publishing House.

Chen, J.S. and Tian, M. (2017). The formation, implementation and influence of The Belt and Road Initiative. CPC History Studies, 2017 (02): 5-13.

Chen, Jiagui, Huang Hongwu, and Wang Yanzhong. 2007. Report on the Process of Industrialization of China (1995 - 2005) — Evaluation and Research on the Level of Industrialization in the Province of China. Beijing, PRC: China Social Sciences Publishing House.

Chen, Jiagui. 2009. Report on China's Industrialization (2009). Beijing, PRC: Social Sciences Academic Press.

Chen, Jianan (2017). Several Issues on "Study on the Cohesion of Contemporary China." Journal of Guangdong Institute of Socialism, 2017(03): 99-110.

Chen, Jiangsheng (2014). Chinese strategic issues should be studied after becoming the second-largest economic entity in the world. Studies on Mao Zedong and Deng Xiaoping Theories, 2014 (10): 45-46.

Chen, Wenling, Ren, Haiping (2015). The adjustment and influence of the global strategy in the United States. Globalization, 2015 (2):78-92.

Chen, Xiangyang (2004). The national traditional strategic and cultural resources of China's peaceful rise in the 21st Century. Journal of Jiangnan Institute of Social Sciences, 2004 (4):79-92.

Cheng Zi-Hao. Sincere, honest, preferential, inclusive and common prosperous- Analysis of differences between the Belt and Road Initiative and The Marshall Plan. Chinese & Foreign Entrepreneurs, 2016(5): 261-262

Cheng, Shi (2005). "pendulum" trade policy under American economic hegemonism. China Business Newspaper, 2005(7):64-71.

Cheng, Weiling (2017). Cooperation is still the main theme of economic relations between China and the United States. Outlook Weekly, 2017 (15): 19-30.

Cheng, Z.H. (2016). Sincere, honest, preferential, inclusive and common prosperous- Analysis of differences between the Belt and Road Initiative and The Marshall Plan. Chinese & Foreign Entrepreneurs, 2016 (5): 261-262

Comprehensive Department of Ministry of Commerce of the People's Republic of China (2015). Vision and Actions on Jointly Building Silk Road Economic Belt and 21st-Century Maritime Silk Road, 2015-03-30.

Cui Ling (2017). On the strategic significance of the construction of the Belt and Road Initiative in China. The Guide of Science & Education (electronic version), 2017(22): 232-233.

Daugherty, James, Pfalzgraf, Robert (2003). Theory of International Relations in Controversy. Beijing, PRC: World Knowledge Press.

Deng, Xiaoping(1993). Address to the Third Plenary Meeting of the Central Advisory Board. Selected Works of Deng Xiaoping, Vol. 3:87, Beijing, PRC: People's Publishing House.

Deng, Xiaoping. (1994). Reforming Enterprises with Advanced Technology and Management Methods, Deng Xiaoping Anthology. Beijing, PRC: People's Publishing House.

Deng, Xiaoping. 1993. Making a Success of Special Economic Zones and Open More Cities to Outside World, Deng Xiaoping anthology. Beijing, PRC: People's Publishing House.

Ding, Lihong. (2011). Perfecting Credit System to Resolve Global Financial Crisis. Northern Economy, 2011 (6): 54-55.

Dong, Defu and Su, Yu. (2018). "The Chinese Dream" and "the World Dream" are in a common and win-win situation: An analysis based on the concept of "Community of Shared Future for Mankind." Journal of Jiangsu University (Social Science Edition), 2018, 20 (3): 6-11.

Dong, Xiaolin. (2010). The Construction of the Contemporary Chinese Environmental Sociology. Beijing, PRC: Beijing Social Sciences Academic Press.

Downs, E.(2015). Mission Mostly Accomplished: China's Energy Trade and Investment along the Silk Road Economic Belt， 2015, Mar. 19.

Du, Tongping. (2011). The Treatment of Pollution Caused by Farmers' Production Way and Lifestyle. Economic Research Survey, 2011 (33): 98.

Duan, Shanshan. (2007). How to Deal with the EU's ROHS\WEEE and EuP Environmental Directives. Beijing, PRC: China Standard Press.

Fan, Hao (2018). Cultural consciousness and confidence in modern Chinese ethics and morality. Journal of Southeast University (Philosophy and Social Science), 2018 (1): 5-14&146.

Fan, Hengshan (2017). The important characteristics of the relationship between China and the world in the new era. Leadership Science, 2017 (24): 21-22.

Fan, Y.Y and Zhang, X.H. (2016). The logical generation of the historical evolution of the Belt and Road Initiative. Qinghai Social Sciences, (2): 1-7.

Fan, Ying-Yuan, Zhang Xiao-Hong (2016). The logical generation of the historical evolution of the Belt and Road Initiative. Qinghai Social Sciences, 2016(2): 1-7.

Fang, Bohua, Sun, Chuanfei (2014). A Review of the Research on the World Pattern after the Global Financial Crisis. Journal of the Party

School of the CPC Zhejiang Provincial Committee, 2014,30(04):66-74.

Feng, Tejun (1988). Contemporary World Political Economy and International Relations. Beijing, PRC: Renmin University of China Press.

Feng, Tejun, Song, Xinning (1992). An Introduction to International Politics. Beijing, PRC: China Renmin University Press.

Fu, Xuan (2016). The study of revenue and corvee in Shanbei during the Ming dynasty. China, Yan'an University, 2016: 27-33.

Gao, Guangchun. 2016. Teaching Research of Mobile Communication Technology and Modern Civilization Based on Lecture. Proceedings of 2016 International Conference on Engineering Management, (4): 99-104

Gao, Lili (2018). Study on Cross-cultural Communication Conflicts under Cross-border E-commerce. Journal of Heihe University, Vol. 2018 (3).

Gelpern, Anna (2011). Sovereignty, Accountability, and Wealth Fund Governance Conundrum. Asian Journal of International Law. 2011 (2): 94-107.

Geng, Yanhu. 2017. Deland Development: An Explanation Framework for Rural Environmental Problems. Journal of Nanjing Agricultural University (Social Science), 17(03): 21-30&155-156.

Gilpin, Robert (2007). War and Change in World Politics. Shanghai, PRC: Shanghai People's Publishing House.

Giovannini, M. and Rosansky, L.(1990). Anthropology and Management Consulting: Forging a New Alliance. The American Anthropological Association.

Goldman, A. (1992). Adoption of Supermarket in a Developing Country: The Selective Adoption Phenomenon. European Journal of Marketing, Vol.1992 (16): 1.

Gu, Yumin (2004). The market economy is a double-edged sword. Liberation Daily, 2004(12):46-47.

Guangming Daily. (2015). Historical Review of the Silk Road. Guangming Daily.

Guo, Hongyu. (2014). The current situation of China's economic system reform and its implementation path. Journal of Shanxi Agricultural University (Social Science Edition), 2014 (08): 766-769.

Guo, Xinying. (2014). Research on the Theory and Practice of the Chinese Dream. Young Literator, 2014 (6): 160-160.

Guo, Yanqin, Li, Youlong (2018). Well-known Experts Discuss the Relationship between China and the World in a New Era. Theoretical Horizon, 2018(03):87-88.

Hamilton, D. (1987). Institutional Economics and Consumption. Journal of Economic Issues.

Han, Xu. (2013). Moral lack and path choice of the socialist market economy. Frontier, 2013 (5): 98-100.

Harris, PP. and Moran, R. (1987). Managing Cultural Differences. Houston: Gulf.

He, Lan (2005). China's Foreign Relations after the Cold War. Beijing, PRC: China Communication University Press.

He, Peiling, and Chen, Meiya. 2012. Sustainable Development of Engineering Construction in China. Applied Mechanics and Materials. (209): 117-129.

He, W.D. and Xin, Y.F. (2015). Implications from the Marshall Plan and on the construction of the Belt and Road Initiative. Academic Forum, 38(08): 80-84.

He, Wei-Da, Xin, Yu-Fei. Implications from the Marshall Plan and on the construction of the Belt and Road Initiative. Academic Forum, 2015, 38(08): 80-84.

He, Zhipeng (2011). From "Peace and Development" to "Harmonious Development" -- The Evolution of International Law Values and China's Position Adjustment. Journal of Social Sciences of Jilin University, 2011,51(04):115-123+160.

Heng, Zhanwei (2017). The study of national cultural genes should attach to the core concept. Journal of Historical Science, 2017 (11): 12-16.

Hong, Yousheng., Sun Chan. (2016). The "One Belt and One Road" Initiative and the Transformation of the Current International System -a Comparison with the "Marshall Plan." Journal of Nanjing University (Philosophy, Humanities, Social Sciences), 2016, 53 (6): 28-38.

Hou, Jie (2018). American higher education certification system and the enlightenment. Contemporary Education Science, 2018 (1): 90-94.

Hou, Yanfang. 2017. Research on the Difficult Problems of Environmental Pollution. Studies in Law and Business, (3): 113-122.

Hu, Jintao (2007). Upholding the Great Banner of Socialism with Chinese Characteristics and Strive for a New Victory in Building a well-off Society in an all-round way. Beijing, PRC: People's Publishing House.

Hu, Wenzhong (2010). An Introduction to Intercultural Communication. Beijing: Foreign Language Teaching and Research Press.

Hu, Ying. (2017). The new development of socialism with Chinese characteristics since the 18th National Congress - From "three self-confidence" to "four self-confidence." Journal of Harbin University, 2017, 38 (9): 19-22.

Huan, Xiang (1989). Contemporary World Political and Economic Issues. Beijing, PRC: World Knowledge Press.

Huang, Fengzhi (2003). Information Revolution and Evolution of Contemporary World Patterns. Journal of Social Sciences of Jilin University, 2003(02):69-74.

Huang, Junying (2017). The research and reference to American innovation and entrepreneurship policy. Science & Technology and Economy, 2017 (1): 31-35.

Huang, Qingying, and Shen, Yaolin. (2012). Exploring the construction of four civilizations and the optimization of the ideological and political education environment. Journal of Huaihua University, 2012, 31 (4): 36-38.

IDC (1998). IDC Internet Market Commerce Model. The Industry Standard.

Ji, Douyong (2017). Contemporary Chinese Road: The "Confidence in the Road" Mentality and Determination. Journal of Guizhou University (Social Sciences). 2017(01): 55-61.

Ji, Jinsan (2011). A study on the present situation and strategic countermeasures of regional economic development in Western China. World of Economics, 2011 (4): 53-69.

Jia, Pu-Jing (2017). The new norm of world economy and construction of the Belt and Road Initiative. Frontiers, 2017(09): 21-27.

Jia, Yuxin (1997). Intercultural Communication. Shanghai: Shanghai Foreign Language Education Press.

Jin, Canrong and Zhang, Kunpeng (2018). Constructing Practice-oriented Sustainable Peace: Reanalysis of New Types of Great Power Relations. Pacific Journal, 2018,26(01):34-46.

Jin, L. (2015). The Belt and Road Initiative： Chinese Marshall Plan? International Studies, (1): 88-99.

Jin, Ling (2015). The Belt and Road Initiative： Chinese Marshall Plan? International Studies, 2015(1): 88-99.

Jin, Z., Mason, R. and Yim, PP. (1998). "Bridging US-China Cross-cultural Differences using Internet and Groupware Technologies. Paper presented at the 7th International Association for Management of Technology Annual Conference, Orland, FL.

Keynes, John Maynard (2018). A General Theory of Employment, Interest and Money. New York, NY: Palgrave Macmillan.

Kim, Joy and Chung, Suh-Yong (2012). The Role of the G20 in Governing the Climate Change Regime. International

Environmental Agreements: Politics, Law and Economics. 2012 (4): 67-81.

Lane, Jan-Erik (2010). The Crisis from the Point of View of Evolutionary Economics. International Journal of Social Economics, 2010 (6): 56-67.

Li, Chengjin. (2017). Study on the Environmental Problems and Environmental Protection and Remediation Strategies in Rural Areas. Resources Economization & Environment Protection, 2017 (01): 96-98.

Li, Chunyan and Gao, Ruijing (2013). Research on institutional mechanism design and supporting policies for promoting autonomous innovation in China. Gansu Journal of Theory, 2013 (04): 5-9.

Li, Dongyan (2015). The United Nations and the Maintenance of International Peace and Security.World Economy and Politics, 2015(04):4-22-154.

Li, Keqiang. (2010). Enhancing the endogenous power of economic growth to accelerate the transformation of development mode. Theoretical reference, 2010 (9): 5-5.

Li, Qize, Huang, Ping (2017). Economic Globalization and Income Inequality in Developed Countries. Red Flag Manuscript, 2017(22): 89-100.

Li, Suqin (2009). Financial hegemony, economic virtualization and the occurrence and adjustment of economic imbalance between China and the United States. International Economic and Trade Exploration, 2009(9): 63-68.

Li, Weisheng and Jiang, Xujun (2013). Research on the Precision Marketing Strategy of Electronic Commerce. Research on Development, Vol. 2013(2).

Li, X.H. (2002). multi-polarization, globalization or after hegemony?The international system during and after the transform. Pacific Journal, 2002(01): 54-61.

Li, X.Y. (2017). Problems and solutions of The Belt and Road Initiative. Intertrade， 2017 (4): 4-9.

Li, Xiang-Yang (2017). Problems and solutions of The Belt and Road Initiative. Intertrade， 2017(4): 4-9.

Li, Xiao-Hua (2002). multi-polarization, globalization or after hegemony? —The international system during and after the transform. Pacific Journal, 2002， (01): 54-61.

Li, Y. (2017). Historical thinking and enlightenment of the Belt and Road Initiative. Journal of Fujian Institute of Socialis, 2017 (2): 73-79.

Li, Yi (2017). Historical thinking and enlightenment of the Belt and Road Initiative. Journal of Fujian Institute of Socialism，2017(2): 73-79.

Li, Yihu (1989). Balance Evolution and Nuclear Age. Hangzhou, PRC: Zhejiang People's Publishing House.

Li, You (2017). Research on the position of national image of contemporary China. China, Jinan: Shandong University, 2017: 41-43.

Li, Yuehua. (2012). The Rise of Cultural China and the Chinese Dream. Collection of Leaders, 2012 (1): 24-26.

Lin Jian and Liu Yi-Bo(2017). the Belt and Road Initiative：Risk and countermeasures.China Economic Report，2017(4): 45-48.

Lin Yong-Liang (2017). World significance of the Belt and Road Initiative. Contemporary World，2017(01): 50-53

Lin, J. and Liu, Y.B. (2017). the Belt and Road Initiative：Risk and countermeasures. China Economic Report，2017 (4): 45-48.

Lin, Jun. (2017). Which Should be Invested in Among So Many Countries along "One Belt and One Road." State-owned Enterprises, 2017 (9): 56-58.

Lin, Y.L. (2017). World significance of the Belt and Road Initiative. Contemporary World，2017 (01): 50-53

Lin, Yueqin and Zhou, Wen (2011). BRICS Economic and Social Development Report 2011. Beijing, PRC: Social Sciences Literature Press.

Liu, Feifei and Li, Haibo. (2018). On the integration of the "Community of Shared Future for Mankind" and the "Chinese Dream." Frontier Economy and Culture, 2018 (05): 50-52.

Liu, Guoguang. (2013). On the direction of China's economic system reform before the Third Plenary Session of the Eighteenth Central Committee -- guard against the trend of privatization in the name of marketization. Jianghuai Forum, 2013 (5): 5-8.

Liu, Haiyang. (2012). The ethical perspective of fairness and efficiency under the socialist market economy. Journal of Shangqiu Vocational and Technical College, 2012 (1): 9-10.

Liu, Jian (2009). An Analysis of the Trend of the Strategic Conception of the American Democratic Union. Modern International Relations, 2009 (11): 45-49.

Liu, Jianfei (2008). On the Trend of "Unpolarization" in the World Structure. Modern International Relations, 2008(04):1-5.

Liu, Weidong (2018). "One Belt One Road" Construction and Macroeconomic Geography. Regional Research and Development, 2018,37(02):171-172.

Liu, Xueju, and Liu Xuebing. (2017). Facing Theory and Reality: Environmental Problems in the Process of Globalization. Journal of Hebei Youth Management Cadre Institute, 2017 (1): 40-42.

Liu, Yanchang. (2007). Focusing on China's vested interest groups. Beijing: Party School Press of the Central Committee of the Communist Party of China, 2007:60.

Liu, Yuan and Zhang Xinling. (2018). Research on financing strategy of privately-owned listed enterprises: Empirical analysis based on panel data from 2012 to 2015. Rural Economy and Technology, 2018 (09): 179-180.

Lu Shan - Bing, Liu Xiao-Lei and Yu Shu-Xiu(2015). Comparative study on Chinese strategic investment on Belt and Road Initiative and The Marshall Plan. The Journal of Humanities, 2015(10): 36-43.

Lu, S.B., Liu, X.L. and Yu, S.X. (2015). Comparative study on Chinese strategic investment on Belt and Road Initiative and The Marshall Plan. The Journal of Humanities, 2015 (10): 36-43.

Luo Meng， Shi Ying(2017). Interpretation of Chinese Belt and Road Initiative from the perspective of world political and economic structure. Social Sciences in Xinjiang， 2017(05): 1-7.

Luo, Huiyun (2014). Unipolar, Multipolar, or Infinite? -- Reconsideration of the Current World Situation and Its Development Trends. Journal of Xiangtan University (Philosophy and Social Sciences), 38(01):144-149.

Luo, M. and Shi, Y. (2017). Interpretation of Chinese Belt and Road Initiative from the perspective of world political and economic structure. Social Sciences in Xinjiang， 2017 (05): 1-7.

Ma, Jun (2017). The number of China's trade remedy cases reached a historic high in 2016. China Tendering, 2017 (2):12-13.

Ma, Weicong (2017). The new hegemonism of the United States after the Cold War. Win the Future, 2017 (13): 174-175.

Mao Yan-Hua (2015). Value and contribution to global economic governance of the Belt and Road Initiative. People's Tribune, 2015(09): 31-33.

Marx. (1975). Das Kapital, Volume 1. Beijing: People's Publishing House, 1975:12.

Max, Karl Heinrich. (1979). Machine, Natural Force and the Application of Science, The Complete Works of Marx and Engels. Beijing, PRC: People's Publishing House.

Mcconnell, C R. (2005). Microeconomics: Principles, Problems, and Policies. Economics Principles Problems & Policies, 2005.

Mei, Guanqun (2018). Actively Constructing A System for International Rules of the Belt and Road. Macroeconomic Management, Vol. 2018(9).

Milesheimer, John. (2017). Why does the United States often feel insecure? The Cold War between the United States and the Soviet Union in the eyes of the "father of containment." Collection of Leaders, 2017 (14): 119-123.

Ming, Haiying (2018). Reflections on Cross-cultural Business Communication from the Perspective of A Community with A Shared Future: Interview with Professor Tian Guang, Shantou University.

Ming, Hao. (2015). "One Belt and One Road" and "Community of Human Destiny." Journal of Minzu University of China (Philosophy and Social Sciences Edition), 2015 (6): 23-30.

Mo, Lifeng (2017). The modern meaning of traditional culture. Jiangsu Zhengxie, 2017 (5):33-34.

Mu, Tao. 2013. The Origin, Characteristics and Chinese Experience of Environmental Anthropology. Nationalities Forum, 2013 (9): 24-27.

Muellbauer, J., and Lattimore, R. (1995). The Consumption Function: A Theoretical and Empirical Overview." In Handbook of Applied Economics, edited by H. Pesaran and M. Wickens. Oxford: Blackwell.

Nasser, Syed, Cooke, Graham, Kranzer, Katharina, Norris, Susan, Olliaro, Piero, Ford, Nathan (2015). Strength of Recommendations in WHO Guidelines using GRADE was Associated with Uptake in National Policy. Journal of Clinical Epidemiology, 2015(6): 112-119.

Ni, Shixiong (2001). Contemporary Theory of International Relations. Shanghai, PRC: Fudan University Press.

Nickels, W. and Wood, M. (2000). Marketing: Relationship, Quality, Value. New York, NY: Worth Publishers.

Niu, Luqing. (2016). Agricultural UAV: Prospects and Constraints. New Economic Guide, 2016 (7): 42-48.

Nye, Joseph (1992). Will the United States Lead the World? Beijing, PRC: Military Translation Press.

Ouyang, Feng and Zhou, Weijun (2006). An Analysis of Online Marketing Culture. Jianghan Tribune, Vol. 2006(3).

Peng, Kaifu.(2017). Current Situation of Pesticide Pollution and Environmental Protection Measures. South China Agriculture, 2017 (23): 1-11.

Price, H.B. (1955). Marshall Pan and Its Meaning： An An Independent and Unbiased Appraisal of the Entire Record， Cornell University Press， Ithaca， New York， p.4.

Qiu, Haiping (2017). Study on the New Development Stage of Socialism with Chinese Characteristics from the Perspective of the World Situation and its Changes. Western Forum, 2017,27(05):16-19.

Qiu, Haiping, Zhao, Min (2017). The dollar and the new imperialism under the logic of capital accumulation. Studies on Marxism, 2017 (6): 47-54.

Ren Ping(2009). Contemporary enlightenment of the dialectical view of 'capital criticism' by Marx- Philosophical reflections on the global financial crisis. Philosophical Trends， 2009(04): 5-12.

Ren, Jie. (2018). A community of Shared Future for Mankind: China's program for global governance. Southeast Academy, 2018 (1).

Research Group of China Center for International Economic Exchanges. The Belt and Road create a new era of economic globalization and win-win development. Globalization, Vol.2017(07).

Rhee, Changyong (2011). From Seoul to Cannes: What Has the G20 Delivered So Far? Harvard International Review. 2011(3): 73-82.

Ros, María, Delgado, Miguel, Vila, Amparo (2003). Fuzzy Method to Disclose Behavior Patterns in a Tagged World. Expert Systems With Applications, 2010(4):76-88.

Saunders, C. (2001). Strategy: The Canadian Marketing Report. P&G steps up multicultural commitment: Establishes a dedicated team to pursue ethnic markets in Canada, 2001.

Semmler, Willi, Young, Brigitte (2010). Lost in Temptation of Risk: Financial Market Liberalization, Financial Market Meltdown and Regulatory Reforms. Comparative European Politics. 2010 (3):88-100.

Shen, Dawei, Zhao, Chen (2005). The New Strategic Triangle: The Response of the United States and Europe to the Rise of China. European Studies, 2005(05): 79-92.

Shen, Lisheng (2009). Evaluating the Contribution of Three Components of GDP ("Troika"). Quantitative Economics, Technology, and Economics, 26 (04): 139-151.

Sheng, Ping. (2017). The Development of Environmental Problems. Geography Teaching Reference, 2017 (06): 45-46.

Sinkovics, R. Yamin, M. and Hossinger, M. (2007). Cultural Adaptation in Cross Border E-Commerce: A Study of German Companies. Journal of Electronic Commerce Research, Vol. 2007 (8):4.

Su Chang-He(2016). The academic agenda of relationship theory. World Economics and Politics, 2016(10):29-38.

Su, Ge (2018). There is Change in the Chaos, and there is Governance in the Change - the International Situation in 2017 and China's Diplomacy. The Contemporary world, 2018(01):12-15.
Sun, Chengwu (2018). The nineteen Party's theoretical innovation of Chinese culture construction in the new era. Journal of Beijing Jiaotong University (Social Sciences Edition), 2018 (17): 28-32.
Sun, Dongfang (2012). The Change of Current World Situation and the Diplomatic Strategic Orientation of China's Peaceful Development. Contemporary World and Socialism, 2012(01):104-108.
Sun, Hangsheng. (2011). Research on the transformation and upgrading of China as the "world factory." Industry Development, 2011, (03): 76-78.
Sun, Jian. (2010). The economic system, resource allocation and the model of economic development. Economic System Reform, 2010 (5): 5-11.
Sun, Wensheng. (2004). Note on the Amendment (Draft) to the Land Management Law of the People's Republic of China - Eleventh Meeting of the Standing Committee of the Tenth National People's Congress, 2004.
Tajovsky L.， Krcek M(2009). The Marshall Plan and Its Relation to the Beginning of the Cold War. Prague Papers on the History of International Relations， Prague： Institute of World History， 2009,pp.465—478.
Tang, Huaishan (2017). New thinking on "hide one's light under a bushel, keep a low profile" of diplomatic strategy. Chinese and Foreign Communication, 2017 (37): 58-59.
Tian, Guang and Dai, Qinqin (2014). What the World will be when China becomes No.1. Beijing, PRC: China Wealth Press.
Tian, Guang and Dai, Qinqin and Qi Xiaoguang. (2012). Strategic thoughts on state management based on criticism of the trend of Pan-market theory. Journal of Shijiazhuang College of Economics. 2012 (02): 92-95.
Tian, Guang and Dai, Qinqin. (2012). Criticism of Pan-marketization. Beijing: China Financial and Economic Publishing House, 2012:1.
Tian, Guang and Wang, Yifan (2014). Cross-cultural Issues in Internet Marketing. Journal of the Second Northwest University for Nationalities, Vol. 2014 (1).
Trabelsi, Mohamed (2011). The Impact of the Financial Crisis on the Global Economy: Can the Islamic Financial System Help? The Journal of Risk Finance. 2011 (1): 111-124.
Trejo, Kristal, Clempner Julio, and Poznyak, Alexander. (2017). Computing the strong – Nash equilibrium for Markov chain games:

Convergence and uniqueness. Applied Mathematical Modelling, 2017,41.

Wallace, Jarryd, Norton, Kevin (2014). Evolution of World Cup Soccer Final Games 1966–2010: Game Structure, Speed and Play Patterns. Journal of Science and Medicine in Sport, 2014(2): 91-102.

Wang Da， Xiang Wei-Xing. The significance of Asian investment Bank on global financial governance, related challenges and China's countermeasures. International Review， 2015(05): 71-81.

Wang Li-Yuan et al. Cultural exchange and mutual learning： promote interconnection between hearts under The Belt and Road Initiative [EB/OL]. Chinese Culture New Agency， 2017-05-16.

Wang Sheng-Sheng, Li Bang-Xi. Periodical alternation or historical transcendence? -a historical orientation of The Belt and Road Initiative from the perspective of changes in the world system. Open Times， 2017(2): 82-94.

Wang Siji (2020) evaluates the fundamental change of the US-China policy. China International Strategy Review, 2020 (1): 1-7.

Wang Yi (2014). Overview of: a harvest year for China's diplomacy. International Studies， 2015(01): 1-10.

Wang Yi-Wei (2015). The Belt and Road Initiative is never the Chinese Marshall Plan. QIUSHI， 2015(12): 55-56.

Wang Yi-Wei (2017). Opportunities and challenges for the Belt and Road Initiative. The Forum of Leadership Science, 2017(12): 3-19.

Wang, D. and Xiang, W.X. (2015). The significance of Asian investment Bank on global financial governance, related challenges and China's countermeasures. International Review， 2015 (05): 71-81.

Wang, Dongjing. (2019). Establishing a socialist market economic system is a great creation. Wisdom China, 2019 (01): 55-57.

Wang, Hao, and Mao Zhu. (2011). The Risk Evaluation and Emergent Monitoring on Environmental Pollution Incidents. Super Science, 2011 (7): 112-127.

Wang, Hong, Yang Niyun, and Yan Zhenguang. (2011). Study on the Evaluation of Persistent, Bio-accumulative and Toxic (PBT) Chemicals in China. Journal of Environmental Engineering Technology. 2011 (5): 414-419.

Wang, Huning (1993). Culture as a nation's strength: soft power. Fudan Journal, 1993 (2): 82-99.

Wang, L.Y.(2017). Cultural exchange and mutual learning： promote interconnection between hearts under The Belt and Road Initiative. Chinese Culture New Agency， 2017-05-16.

Wang, Lin and Zhu, Jiemei (2017). Review of "From closed to open: China early modernization and social transformation." Journal of Historical Science. 2017(3):121-124.

Wang, S.S. and Li, B.X. (2017). Periodical alternation or historical transcendence? -a historical orientation of The Belt and Road Initiative from the perspective of changes in the world system. Open Times， 2017 (2): 82-94.

Wang, Shiran (2018). On the post-Cold War world pattern. Talents, 2018(02):p.194-196.

Wang, Tianjin, and Tian, Guang. (2012). Environmental Anthropology. Yinchuan, PRC: Ningxia People's Publishing House.

Wang, Xinbo and Wei, Tao (2009). The pattern of international relations and China's peaceful rise. Learning Theory, 2009 (27): 55-56.

Wang, Y. (2015). Overview of 2014: A harvest year for China's diplomacy. International Studies， 2015 (01): 1-10.

Wang, Y.W. (2015). The Belt and Road Initiative is never the Chinese Marshall Plan. QIUSHI， 2015 (12): 55-56.

Wang, Y.W. (2017). Opportunities and challenges for the Belt and Road Initiative. The Forum of Leadership Science, 2017 (12): 3-19.

Wang, Yongli (2018). Ten Years of the Global Financial Crisis. Chinese SMEs, 2018(03):64-67.

Wang, Youcai and Li, Xiaomin (1987). Postwar World Political Economy and International Relations. Harbin, PRC: Heilongjiang People's Publishing House.

Warner, F. (1997). Nike tones town bad-boy image to boost sales in China's market. The Wall Street Journal Interactive Edition.

Weng, Yongxi (2018). A Dialogue between Weng Yongxi and an American Official. https://server.9yuntu.cn/doc/8zlsKXtsSJY0wR0T53yFZD?yuntuFrom=qq34

Wolfinbarger, M.F. and Gilly, M.C., (2005), Consumer behavior. In the Internet Encyclopedia, H. Bidgoli (Ed.), Vol.2005 (1) (Hoboken, NJ: John Wiley).

Wouters, Jan and Ramopoulos, Thomas (2012). The G20 and Global Economic Governance: Lessons from Multi-Level European Governance? Journal of International Economic Law. 2012 (3): 92-103.

Wu, Jiapei (2000). Net Economy and Its Influence on Economic Theory. Academic Research, Vol. 2000(1).

Wu, Wen and Zheng, Hang (2012). A Study on the Impact of Cultural Differences on E-Commerce Activities. Journal of Chongqing

University of Science and Technology (Social Sciences Edition), Vol. 2012(6).

Xi Jin-Ping(2017). Secure a decisive victory in building a moderately prosperous society in all respects and strive for the great success of socialism with Chinese characteristics for a new era—Delivered at the 19th National Congress of the Communist Party of China. Beijing: the 19th National Congress of the Communist Party of China, 2017.

Xi Jin-Ping.(2015) Marching towards a community of shared destiny and creating a new future for Asia Science &Technology Industry of China, 2015(04): 8-9.

Xi, J.P. (2015). Marching towards a community of shared destiny and creating a new future for Asia Science &Technology Industry of China, 2015(04): 8-9.

Xia Xian-Liang (2016). The Belt and Road Initiative and a new world economic system . Frontier's, 2016(9): 56-75.

Xia Xian-Liang (2017). Brilliant achievements of The Belt and Road Initiative in more than three.Foreign Investment in China, 2017(6): 26-27.

Xia, Luran (2018). The cultural confidence and cultural consciousness proposed in the Belt and Road initiative. Enterprise Reform and Management, 2018 (1):179-180.

Xia, X.L. (2016). The Belt and Road Initiative and a new world economic system. Frontier's, 2016 (9): 56-75.

Xia, X.L. (2017). Brilliant achievements of The Belt and Road Initiative in more than three. Foreign Investment in China, 2017 (6): 26-27.

Xiao Cao (2017). Historical changes of the Belt and Road Initiative. CPC Party members (He Bei), 2017(12): 18-19.

Xiao, Xi (2015). China's Peaceful Development Road: Cultural Foundation, Strategic Orientation and Practical Significance. International Observations, 2015(04):1-21.

Xie, Di and Xie, Siru. (2014). An Economic Analysis of the Chinese Dream. Economist. 2014 (01): 14-21.

Xu, Fei (2017). The other view of science and culture – Why is Science walking with Democracy. Impact of Science on Society, 2017 (2): 12-19.

Xu, Jialin (2018). New Trends in World Development and New Objectives of China's International Strategy. Foreign Social Sciences, 2018(01):32-34.

Xu, Mingqi. (2006). The Impact of the Expanding Gap Between the Payments and Current Account Deficit of the United States on the World Economy. International Financial Research, 2006 (4): 38-43.

Xu, Xin (2001). The Collapse of Superpowers. Beijing, PRC: Social Sciences Academic Press.

Xue, Anwei (2018). A Well-Revivaled World Economy: New Patterns, New Risks, and New Motive Forces -- A World Economic Analysis Report of 2018.World Economy Research, 2018(01):3-19.

Yan, Xuetong (1997). International environmental assessment of China's rise. Strategy and Management, 1997 (1): 66-81.

Yang, Dongping. (2007): The Transformation and Game of China's Environment. Beijing, China: Social Sciences Academic Press.

Yang, Qiyu. (2016). Pan-marketization and moral dilemma. Mao Zedong and Deng Xiaoping Theory Research, 2016 (4): 44-47.

Yin, Xiaolin and Yang, Wen (2011). The IMF predicts that China's economy will surpass that of the United States for five years, drawing attention from foreign media. Law System Evening News, 2011 (5):12-13.

Yu, Lin. (2010). The impact of technological innovation on the trade competitiveness of high-tech products. Forum on Statistics and Information, 2010, 25 (5): 76-80.

Yu, Yun (2005). The new trend of the world situation. Outlook News Weekly, May 8, 2005.

Yu, Zhengliang (2000). The Global Pattern of the New Century in the Process of Economic Globalization.Fudan Journal (Social Sciences), 2000(01):1-6.

Yu, Zhongfu (2018). Carrying out Xi Jinping's thought of a strong army in an all-round way, running the armed forces by law furtherly. Ideological and Political Education Research, 2018 (1): 12-14.

Zeng, Jianwen, and Sun, Yanjing (2011). Industrialization Progress and Resource Environmental Energy Saving. Beijing, PRC: China Machine Press.

Zenn, Jacob. (2015). "Future Scenarios on the New Silk Road: Security, Strategy, and the SCO."

Zhai, K. (2015). Strategic thinking on The Belt and Road Initiative. International Review，2015(4):49-60.

Zhang Jian-Xin(2012). The post-Western international system and the rise of the East. World Economics and Politics, 2012(05): 4-20.

Zhang Ke-Yun and Deng Zhong-Liang.(2017) Construction logic for regional cooperation's framework under the Belt and Road Initiative. China Opening Herald，2017(2): 17-22.

Zhang, Feinan(2017). The Theoretical Paradigm of Contemporary China's Environmental Research. Journal of Nanjing University of Technology (Social Science), 2017 (03): 81-88.

Zhang, J.X. (2012). The post-Western international system and the rise of the East. World Economics and Politics, (05): 4-20.

Zhang, K.Y. and Deng, Z.L. (2017). Construction logic for international cooperation's framework under the Belt and Road Initiative. China Opening Herald, 2017 (2): 17-22.

Zhang, Minqian (2001). American Foreign Economic Strategy. Beijing, PRC: World Knowledge Press.

Zhang, Muzhi (2017). The propaganda and historical significance of the American prisoners of war in the American Revolution. World History, 2017 (5): 61-78.

Zhang, Ping, Nong Lin, and Han Jingyu. (2017). The Evolution, Development and Transformation of Environmental Policy in China. Journal of CUG (Social Science). 2017 (06): 105-116.

Zhang, Wen. (2013). Research on Environmental Anthropology in the Past Hundred Years. Journal of Guangxi National University (Philosophical Social Science), 35(6): 53-59.

Zhang, Xinmin and Jiang, Qing (2011). Confucianism and the Politics of Kings: A Dialogue on the Development of modernity in the study of the outside King. The Yangming Annual Academic Journal, 2011 (3):69-83.

Zhang, Yonghong. (2017). Yin Wengui. Generation, value and realization of the concept of "Community of Shared Future for Mankind." Ideological and Theoretical Education, 2017 (08): 33-39.

Zhang, Yuguo (2017). Trump regime and the American Asia Pacific rebalance strategy. Northeast Asia Forum, 2017 (2):13-24.

Zhang, Zhongtao. (2005). Corruption and Anti-corruption in the Perspective of the Institution. Hubei Social Science, 2005 (11): 44-46.

Zhao, Congxian. (1980). The Collapse of the Capitalist World Monetary System from the Gold Standard to the Dollar-centered. Journal of Lanzhou University, 1980(2): 4-13.

Zhao, Jingfang (2012). Four strategic misunderstandings in the context of China's peaceful rise. China Review, 2012 (10): 24-25.

Zhao, Jingfang (2012). The Reasons for the Misreading of China's Peaceful Rise. Study Monthly. 2012(19):39-39.

Zhao, Kejin. (2016). The "One Belt and One Road" Which Leads to the Destiny of Human Community. Contemporary World, 2016 (6): 9-13.

Zhao, Yingmin, and Ren Guanping. (2012). The 11th Five-Year Environmental Protection Science and Technology Award Assembly. Beijing, PRC: China Environmental Science Press.

Zhen, Cuimin (2017). An Analysis of the Relations between the Components of National Cohesion in Contemporary China. Journal of North China University of Technology (Social Sciences), 2017(06): 81-90.

Zheng, Jinping (2017). Reflection on the construction of harmonious culture and the promotion of national cultural soft power. Think Tank Era, 2017 (11): 293-295.

Zhou, Bajun. (1984). The Zigzag International Exchange Rate System -- On the Evolution of the International Monetary Fund's View on the International Exchange Rate System. World Economic Research, 1984 (3): 12-14.

Zhou, Hong and Yang, Xiaolei (2011). An Overview of Innovation Studies on Cross-cultural Online Consumers. Economy, Vol. 2011 (337).

Zhu, Wenbo (2015). Study on the Chinese Cross Border E-commerce under the Background of One Belt and One Road with Guangdong Province for Example. Guangdong University of Foreign Studies.

Zhu, Xiangdong and Bei, Qinghua (2008). A critical outline of the official standard. Journal of Central South University, 2008(4): 379-482.

Zou, Dahai (2017). A new probe into the book age of the Nine Chapters on the Mathematical Art and quantity system during the Qin and Han Dynasties – Research on archaeological materials based on cultural relics. Studies in History of Natural Science, 2017 (3): 293-315.

Index

About the Authors

Dr. Tian Guang currently serves as a specially appointed professor at School of Business, Huaihua University. He also serves as the Dean of Advanced Research Institute for Applied Anthropology at Jishou University and the Doctoral Supervisor at Hebei University. Dr. Tian received his Ph. D. in social anthropology from York University in 1995 and an MBA from Wilfried Laurier University in 1999. Dr. Tian authored and co-authored 25 books and published over a hundred peer-reviewed academic articles. His research interesting is in regional development, cross-cultural marketing management, and economic anthropology.

Dr. Chen Gang is currently Chair Professor and Director of Center for Social and Economic Behavior Studies at Yunnan University of Finance and Economics in China, and Chief Editor of International Journal of Business Anthropology. He received a MA in anthropology from Iowa State University in the US in August 1993 and a Ph.D. in anthropology from Ohio State University in the US in June 2000. He used to work as a lecturer in Xi'an Jiaotong University (1983-1990), a post-doc research fellow in the Department of Human Nutrition at The Ohio State University (2000-2004), visiting professor in Department of Sociology and Anthropology of Ohio University (2004-2006). His chief research interests are in the areas of business anthropology, food safety and culture, development anthropology and cultural tourism, globalization and culture change. He has received numerous research grants both in the US and in China. So far, he has published a large number of academic papers and books both in Chinese and English.

Made in the USA
Monee, IL
05 November 2026

67808626R00128